Rural Education History

STUDIES IN URBAN–RURAL DYNAMICS

Series Editors
Gregory M. Fulkerson and Alexander R. Thomas, SUNY Oneonta

This series focuses attention on understanding theoretically and historically the development and maintenance of Urban–Rural Systems through a spatial, demographic, and ecological perspective. It seeks a blending or reintegration of the urban, rural, and environmental research literatures under a comprehensive theoretical paradigm. As such, we further specify Urban–Rural Dynamics as analysis of human population distribution on social variables, including politics, economics, and culture.

Recent Titles in Series

Rural Education History: State Policy Meets Local Implementation, by Casey Thomas Jakubowski

Country Teachers in City Schools: The Challenge of Negotiating Identity and Place, by Chea Parton

Community Change and Development: An Urban-Rural Dynamics Approach, by Gregory M. Fulkerson

City and Country: The Historical Evolution of Urban-Rural Systems, by Alexander R. Thomas and Gregory M. Fulkerson

The Rural Primitive in American Popular Culture: All Too Familiar, by Karen E. Hayden

Urban Dependency: The Inescapable Reality of the Energy Economy, by Gregory M. Fulkerson and Alexander R. Thomas

Urbanormativity: Reality, Representation, and Everyday Life, by Alexander R. Thomas and Gregory M. Fulkerson

Rural Voices: Language, Identity and Social Change across Place, edited by Elizabeth Seale and Christine Mallinson

Reinventing Rural: New Realities in an Urbanizing World, edited by Alexander R. Thomas and Gregory M. Fulkerson

Reimagining Rural: Urbanormative Portrayals of Rural Life, edited by Gregory M. Fulkerson and Alexander R. Thomas

Rural Education History

State Policy Meets Local Implementation

Casey Thomas Jakubowski

LEXINGTON BOOKS
Lanham • Boulder • New York • London

Published by Lexington Books
An imprint of The Rowman & Littlefield Publishing Group, Inc.
4501 Forbes Boulevard, Suite 200, Lanham, Maryland 20706
www.rowman.com

86-90 Paul Street, London EC2A 4NE

Copyright © 2023 by The Rowman & Littlefield Publishing Group, Inc.

All rights reserved. No part of this book may be reproduced in any form or by any electronic or mechanical means, including information storage and retrieval systems, without written permission from the publisher, except by a reviewer who may quote passages in a review.

British Library Cataloguing in Publication Information Available

Library of Congress Cataloging-in-Publication Data

Names: Jakubowski, Casey Thomas, author.
Title: Rural education history : state policy meets local implementation / Casey Thomas Jakubowski.
Description: Lanham, Maryland : Lexington Books, 2023. | Series: Studies in urban-rural dynamics | Includes bibliographical references and index.
Identifiers: LCCN 2023010629 (print) | LCCN 2023010630 (ebook) | ISBN 9781666929935 (cloth) | ISBN 9781666929942 (ebook)
Subjects: LCSH: Education, Rural--New York (State)--History. | Rural schools--New York (State)--History. | Education and state--New York (State)--History.
Classification: LCC LC5147.N4 J35 2023 (print) | LCC LC5147.N4 (ebook) | DDC 370.9173/409747--dc23/eng/20230322
LC record available at https://lccn.loc.gov/2023010629
LC ebook record available at https://lccn.loc.gov/2023010630

∞™ The paper used in this publication meets the minimum requirements of American National Standard for Information Sciences—Permanence of Paper for Printed Library Materials, ANSI/NISO Z39.48-1992.

*For my parents, family, and my friends.
For my students, past, present, and future.
For all those who see rural areas as their balance.
My grandmother, Catherine Mauler, so desperately
wanted to teach. You inspired me!*

Contents

Introduction	1
Chapter 1: Problem Definition in Rural New York	13
Chapter 2: The "Hidden Narrative"	35
Chapter 3: Lakeside Conflict	51
Chapter 4: Leadership's Dissonance on School Reform	59
Chapter 5: State of the State for Rural New York	75
Chapter 6: The Decayed Community: Losing Schools in Rural New York State	93
Chapter 7: Is New York Unique?	105
Conclusion: What Should We Do from Here?	115
References	119
Index	145
About the Author	151

Introduction

In Fulkerson and Thomas (2019) seminal work on sociology of relationships between rural and urban America, the term urbanormativy was created. The scholars created the term to pinpoint how researchers, and the popular media describe their world views through enhancing urban viewpoints. By doing so, rural education has been problematized (Biddle et al., 2019; Williams and Tieken, 2021). I personally experienced this as a practitioner educator, during my career as a member of the State Education Government (Ellis et al., 2011; Jakubowski, 2021), and active consumer of news concerning rural America. Practicing education in what many people perceive as an urban state, such as New York, I have observed urbanormativy at play frequently, and with profoundly, and inherently poor outcomes for rural areas (Appalachian Regional Commission, 2022; Jakubowski, 2020a; Jakubowski, 2021). Quite often the needs and the realities of rural communities are often forgotten or are seconded or reduced in favor of urban normative or metro centric activities, policies, or plans. It is my opinion that these over 100-year policies and practices have resulted in rage in the rural areas, and open opposition, and near rebellion against the urban normative and metro centric policies (Longhurst, 2020) which, in rural resident's worldviews have detracted, and disadvantaged their lives in contrast to the urban residents. This book investigates the over 100 year policy of urbanormativy through the lens of rural policy, theoretically designed as school improvement through exemplary case studies (Stake, 1995). The unique examples of these case studies tie history, policy analysis, and local actions to the events in the capitol and at home.

While attention in the 2020s has focused on the election in 2016 of President Donald Trump, the 2020 campaign for president, and the January 6, 2021, Washington DC Capitol building insurrection to attempt to overthrow the lawful election of President Joe Biden, scholars and popular media are trying to understand why rural Americans feel so disenfranchised (Longhurst, 2020). The second example of the rebellious nature of rural Americans are the numerous battle flags of the Northern Tennessee Army of the Confederacy. Rural residents fly this flag in the open, and proudly in many instances. Why NASCAR and other southern and rural cultural groups have denounced the use of the flag, rural people and populations embrace it as a symbol of their "heritage" (Loewen, 2021). As described in Lowenthal's (1998) book, most historical memories in groups not affiliated with professional history, and many people who do not study history, see the past as "heritage" which is promoted as a positive interpretation of history in order to allow people to "feel good" about some aspect of their shared past. Heritage is related closely to boosterism, unabashed patriotism, and other uncritical reviews of the past and the influences people had upon the events, actions, and consequences. Heritage is useful to bring tourists, but we must remember, as practitioners, identifying and describing the negative or complex parts of history and education are crucial as well (Wallace, 1996).

Some very important works, including Catte (2018); Cramer (2016); Wuthnow (2019) have taken a nuanced approach to rural communities. In these exceptional works, the authors examined and addressed common issues in rural America, by first and foremost talking to rural Americans. Second, their works described through these interactions some significant issues rural Americans feel are being overlooked by more urban reformers, government officials, and the press. In well executed research studies, the authors, an historian, a political scientist, and a sociologist examined the intersection of the three areas of "community study" buy examining specifically the why, what, and how of the folkways that rural people value, practice, and center at their identities which urban people in the areas of government and media do not seem to understand.

This book brings together recent research, historical events, and policy analysis in an effort to describe the antecedents of the rural realities, and specifically how in New York State, power shifted from the rural areas to more urban focused priorities.

RECENT RESEARCH

A recent addition to the education literature, by Howley and Redding (2021), provides practitioners an informative, and extensively researched work on rural education. The work identifies and describes not just the theory, but the practice of rural education. Their work starts out with a crucial and important memory for researchers: "rural areas are not homogenous" (p. 3). This theme is critical for researchers, students, policymakers, and the media to remember. The book builds on the idea that uniqueness is crucial and transformational to ensure that rural areas receive specific and actionable assistance which is relevant to the specific area.

A significant and engaging book, which is in my opinion, one of the most comprehensive explorations of rural education in the United States, has just been published (Azano, Eppley and Biddle, 2021). In this edited volume, a thorough examination of four major themes, in detail, is addressed to students, researchers, and practitioners. The work starts with a definition and history of rural education research, exploring how the field identifies and creates the narrative of the field. The work critiques the definitions, traditions, and techniques of defining rural. The introductory chapters of the book are a master class for students, researchers, and frankly the media and policy makers on the debates in the areas of rural education. The work then moves into exploring rural communities, their schools, and how the symbiotic, or difficult, relationships between the two evolve and change. The exploration of communities utilizes several scholarly traditions and frameworks and provides clear understandings and roadmaps to people interested in rural America. The next major section examines curriculum studies in, for, and about rural areas. Exploring what, how, and why different areas of national, state, and local standards are taught, as well as ancillary but critical areas of student and teacher supports describes the current and the envisioned ways in which rural education can grow and change. The fourth and final section is the identity and equity section. This fourth critical area really explains and defines how rural areas see themselves, and what are some of the good and the bad with rural areas educational programs. Keeping with the truth that "when you see one rural community, you have seen one rural community" the section clearly finds a frank, and highly engaging way to ensure researchers, policymakers, and if utilized, media can tell the rural narrative correctly.

As one of the leading lights in rural education described in his address (Corbett, 2021) rural educational research must become recentered, and reprioritized by researchers and policy makers. I added media to this list. Corbett (2021) points out, rural is currently defined by place, as in a relationship to not urban. With the preoccupation with space, place, and othering in most research, policy, and media, there exists frequent misunderstandings, and critically abrasive policy and media decisions which reduce rural residents to tropes or caricatures lacking the depth and breadth of their actual existence (Lennon, 2021). Corbett (2021) finds frequently there is little true authenticity in the research undertaken on rural education, for most outsiders are urban, and proclaim, and hew to the deficit model which has a 100-year history in the research on and media reporting of, rural areas. Corbett (2021) reminds researchers, academics, and others to ensure that each rural area is treated as unique.

An important study demonstrated that the Northeast rural areas of the United States are underrepresented within academic research. This book is designed to meet the call that Thier et al. (2021) gave to researchers to examine or consider two major points. First, identify the areas in which the research is situated. Second, consider examining in detail unique areas in the northeastern United States, which has rural schools and districts, but is often overlooked as too urban. While New York, Massachusetts, Pennsylvania, and the rest of the Mid Atlantic and New England are urbanized, the "spaces in between" are rural. National Clearinghouse of Educational Statistics (NCES, 2011) identifies more than 40 percent of school districts in New York State as rural. As the New York State Center for Rural Schools (Sipple, ND) has shown, research into rural New York is often lagging, or as I have found in my work (Jakubowski, unpublished) the research is part of unpublished dissertations, master's thesis, or other academic work not widely distributed.

An unfortunate reality exists that calls to examine rural areas in a more systematic way are not new. Rather, just re-energized after the 2021 Capitol riot (Longhurst, 2020). The narrative, or what historians call the historiography, of rural education has deep roots (Biddle and Azano, 2016). Most recently, Anthony-Stevens and Langford (2020) described their research and course instruction to ensure that rural pre-service teachers were aware of diversity within rural context, as rural communities are significantly more diverse than the general perception of white farming communities in bubbles. The theme of acknowledging diversity continues with a study on rural uniqueness continues with Corbett and Gereluk (2020) book on preparing rural teachers in Canada and honoring First Nations culture and history. This is timely, and should be critically examined by United States scholars, especially considering the tragedy of the Canadian and American schools designed to genocide native peoples. The theme extends into a timely article on research practice by Thier et al. (2020) which examines, and offers suggestions to ensure that researchers working in rural and non-rural settings do not "disappear" rural uniqueness as they disaggregate data. Three suggestions out of the research are worth quoting:

> First, we recommend incorporating geographic locale into analyses, whenever possible: this school characteristic may explain variance in policy- and practice-relevant outcomes. Second, when incorporating geographic locale, it should be operationalized precisely using relevant theory as a guide. Third, a polytomous approach is less likely to obscure inherent variation rather than dichotomizing geographic locale. The latter might confound findings and imperil decision making. (Thier et al., 2020 p. 13)

Thier et al. (2020) identified the major problem facing many rural researchers: the lack of clear classification of what, exactly, is rural. In current parlance, many researchers rely on the United States government for a population-based classification (NCES, 2022). Colloquially, many researchers, and often the popular media describe rural as "not urban." Often the conceptualization of rural areas includes decentralized populations, resource extraction communities engaged in pastoral work or timbering, mining, or tourism of recreation. This echoes earlier works by Duncan (1999) and the recently published work by Sherman (2021). In their work, fundamental to rural research, both authors reported on how the haves and the have nots in rural America are often clearly divisible. Both authors found that rural Americans often need to rely on "informal" economies of trade, barter, and under the table work in order to survive. There is also, both authors found, a significant current of "deserving people" mentality which divides the rural communities into those who give charity to people who are deemed as deserving, and those who do not deserve charity because they are unworthy.

IS RURAL IMPORTANT?

As Corbett (2014) found in a research study, a trope of rural peace and community harmony exists in many people's idealizations and reporting on rural areas. There is often divisiveness in rural areas and communities. Demographic, economic, and political policy enacted have often created significant disagreements in rural areas (Jakubowski, 2019). The harmony trope often leads to reporting and research into areas when an unusual circumstance, or a conflict raises to the level of catching journalists (Dearing and Rodgers, 1996) or researcher's attention (Stake, 1995). The harmony trope also skews the urban and suburban focused policy maker's understanding of the unique needs of rural America. Therefore, legislation and policies are created which, intentionally or not, disadvantages rural Americans (Schafft, 2016).

Another recent study (Seelig, 2021) advanced rural research further by finding many researchers, in their methodologies designed to anonymize research settings, are erasing rural areas. In the research study, Seelig (2021) reinforced Cervone's (2017) research on neo-liberal reforms designed to repress rural educational establishments, and place-based knowledge as irrelevant to the capitol based, humans as consumers and workers within the United State's current educational system. Cervone's (2017) and Seelig's (2021) studies echo work from Thomas (2005) concerning the destruction of multiple rural communities in upstate New York in order to create a water reservation for New York City. When local communities are literally erased, or in policy, ignored in the local resident's perceptions, anger begins to build (Wuthnow, 2018). In New York State, as an urban normative state, residents have cited for close to 70 years a feeling of being left behind in multiple different areas of policy (Osterud, 2012).

Additional research confirms the lack of research into rural areas, and a significant over reporting of urban areas. Thier and Beach (2019) discovered that geographic locales are often not reported in research among journals.

Within this context, the researchers also found that the many major research journals often privilege urban research over all other types. Their findings echo what Johnson et al. (2021) found in their research, namely

> Nearly one in five U.S. students attends a rural school, yet we know very little about achievement, achievement gaps, and academic growth in those schools, especially differences between school year and summer changes in achievement. This lack of evidence is troubling. (Johnson et al., 2021)

With the increased emphasis on how researchers and media "know very little about . . . those schools" (Johnson et al., 2021), the question remains why, and how do the academics and popular media continue to refrain from researching rural areas?

JOURNEY TO THE BOOK

My own personal journey is part of what Schulte and Walker-Gibbs (2016) called self-studies; this project started with an initial exploration during my master's program at Binghamton University into the history of Little Valley Central School District's attempts at consolidation over 50 years. As part of a master's project, I sought to try and understand my personal experiences as a young teacher in this district which no longer exists having been consolidated into a new larger school system. Historians often look at the documents relating to the consolidation process from times before World War II and yet now after almost 50 years approaching 60 years, we need to start thinking about the current state of rural research especially in school districts that are in predominantly metro states such as New York.

A second potential theoretic lens is the autoethnographic lens (Ellis et al., 2011). Autoethnography is

> an approach to research and writing that seeks to describe and systematically analyze personal experience in order to understand cultural experience. This approach challenges canonical ways of doing research and representing others and treats research as a political, socially-just and socially-conscious act. A researcher uses tenets of autobiography and ethnography to do and write autoethnography. (Ellis et al., 2011, p. 273)

Beginning to think about policies both political as well as sociological during my PhD coursework, I began to realize the portrayal of rural education in research and popular media is critical to understanding the rural-urban divide that Theobald (2017) as well as others have reported on. This work is in critique of what many researchers and popular media portray as backwardness, sub optimization, and other tropes. In my opinion, there is a real cultural war between the researchers, popular media, policy makers, and rural communities and residents' experiences are recorded, researched, and reported.

I experienced situations during my work in rural areas where teachers talked down about, or to, the rural students attending school (Carr and Kefalas, 2009). This reality echoed what researchers have found about teachers in some rural areas. As Panos and Seelig (2019) found, teachers in rural areas often have two significant impacts on rural students. First, narratives in rural areas often

> reveals a distinct refutation of the neoliberal poverty and education discourses that declare human capital development and free market competition to be the end goals of educational and economic policies . . . teachers' discourse on poverty reaffirms common stereotypes of poor people (Gorski, 2008), including that poor parents do not value education, abuse alcohol and/or drugs, lack work ethic, and are "linguistically deficient". . . . rurality is both a spatial denotation and an identifying characteristic, but it is not a static construct . . . our study indicates that the work of placing the intersections of broad discourses of rurality, poverty, and schooling both discredits and affirms these discourses and is part of concrete actionable choices on the part of educators. (Panos and Seelig, 2019, pp. 34–35)

From the practitioner, researcher, policy makers, and reporter's ethical perspective rural life should be portrayed as authentically as possible based upon whatever research schema you are utilizing (Biddle et al., 2019). In academia, we try to create theories, patterns, and generalizations from a series of events to demonstrate the applicability of individual events to an overall generalization (Stake, 1995). Academics, and journalists want to reveal broad patterns of human existence by selecting stories and events that will illustrate broader patterns for their readers. Ethnographic researchers, and others interested in researching people and events are trying to develop what is described as "thick descriptions" of events and understandings. Thick description (Ponterotto, 2006) is defined as "involves understanding and absorbing the context of the situation or behavior. It also involves ascribing present and future intentionality to the behavior" (p. 539). Ponterotto (2006) reaffirms the significance of thick descriptions of the contextuality, participants, their rationales, and reasons as significant and relevant, and necessary to enhancing and properly recording research within communities.

This book should help eliminate what Clark (2014) describes as the nostalgic trap many researchers and media members fall into when examining rural America. Clark (2014), and other scholars have identified a trope of peaceful little red schoolhouses in a summery grass filled meadow at the crossroads in a quiet country area. Rural areas and people are complex, and each area and peoples are unique. The portrait of idyllic, and sameness removes the agency, or ability of individuals and communities in rural areas to demonstrate their uniqueness. As the chapters in the book demonstrate, the monolithic portrayals often create policy which reduces rural areas to almost caricatures.

I frame this work with the use of ethnography and subaltern research, as the two combine and entwine, allowing us to research into the "hidden narratives" which Scott (1990) describes in a theory of sociology and policy. In my research (Jakubowski, 2019) into educational policy implementation in rural areas, I found that a significant amount of research into rural areas favored the elite, including school board members, school administrators, and local power holders. The research often ignored what local people, or subalterns, who, as individuals without formal or informal power, wanted or thought. Using what Cramer (2016) described as listening to people in informal settings, I found, and supported the research which Cramer (2016) reported, namely that rural people who are not in power often disagree with what their local community leaders, state and federal officials believe as "necessary." This echoes what Rey, (2014) and Tangorra (2013) discovered in their research into rural superintendents as brokers between federal, state, and local officials and the people.

We also tend to forget a significant issue, that of ego during research interviews. Elites within a community want to portray everyday life as something which they benevolently helped to improve. Assuring their position, or legacy, or legitimacy to outsiders usually means demonstrating that a local community is in good stead (Tieken, 2014). Elites within a rural community are often large business owners, large landowners, the superintendent of schools, the principal, the police or fire chief, as well as the mayor. These elites seek to ensure the village continues in ways that allow them to maintain their status as the leaders. With globalization on the horizon as Brown and Schafft (2011) describe in their book the isolation and self-sustaining ecology of these communities is on its way to ending. No longer is a local business or agency the largest controller of jobs or businesses to the outside world. Conglomerates merged businesses, banks, and state governments to push the stability of these main streets into a worldwide system where decisions are made across the ocean (Doukas, 2003). If a community is lagging in economic, social, political, and educational measures, then how can the local leadership not in some way be responsible? As Tieken (2014) pointed out, when we anonymize research in areas, we forget that publicly elected and appointed officials are just that: public.

As I describe in my research (Jakubowski, 2019), federal and state accountability measures in the area of education have ramped up two significant areas of educational governance oversight. First, governmental oversight has demanded schools, in general, but rural schools become more efficient in their expenditures of public funds. Second, schools have, since 2001, held accountability for improved effectiveness as defined by student performance on state testing. Within these two issues, efficiency and effectiveness, the silver bullet for improvement since at least 1900, has been school district consolidation. In a "bigger is better" belief, state governments have pushed for consolidation of smaller districts to more closely mirror the urban schools which were heralded as the best and most efficient systems (Tyack and Cuban, 1997). In New York State, the educational policy towards school district management has, since 1958, called for consolidation of small rural districts (Jakubowski, 2020a).

The second major pressure on many rural schools has been the economic crisis, since 2008, which has reduced, in impact, financing and support for especially rural schools (Sipple and Yao, 2015). These realities, greater demand for increased effectiveness, efficiency, and the demand to consolidate has led to existential crises in rural areas. The increased pressure to consolidate on local districts have been told in many other places (Jakubowski, 2019), with stories concerning the critical nature of schools to their communities discussed elsewhere (Casto et al., 2016; Sipple et al., 2019). The very reason many communities have pride in their local schools is its representation of hopes, dreams, and the continued community sacrifice to ensure that their children are ready for the future. When a community can no longer support their school, and their available options are no longer in play, or a consolidation attempt fails, quite often the leadership questions the school district's survival (Steele, 2010).

While elites often control decision making in areas of economics, politics, society growth, and education, another group, the subalterns, their story needs to be explored and published. For everybody else in the community the question becomes how to survive in a changing world when there is no longer agency. Agency has been lost to state and federal government reforms, and as the power of local school boards decreases, many residents, especially in rural areas feel that reforms are ignoring their values, their goals, and worldview (Cramer, 2016; Casto, 2019; Tieken and Auldridge-Reveles, 2019; Wuthnow, 2018). This is an important question to consider, as the United State's federalism tradition, until recently, has cherished and fetishized local control in education. This is especially relevant, as past reform and counter reform movements have struggled towards progressive federal and in some places, state government action, and local reaction which called into question the veracity of the reforms, in order to ensure the local power structure was held intact (Scribner, 2016).

One of the serious examples of rural Americans left behind occurred during the early days of the COVID-19 pandemic, which started in 2020, and resulted in almost nationwide transitions to online, virtual, or remote schooling. In many urban areas, students needed access to computers, the internet, and other materials, which were available due to the presence of broadband access in urban and suburban areas. In rural areas, many residents still do not have access to broadband internet access, primarily due to a lack of infrastructure. Most economic development reports, and media, have covered this need. The lack of broadband internet, or internet in general is limiting educational, economic, and social access for students, businesses, and others in rural areas (Brenner et al., 2020; Patrick et al., 2021).

From the students in the school to the cashiers in the small businesses to the parents struggling to survive, who tells their story? Who ensures their story comes to the forefront?

Ever since the election of 2016 Americans are faced with a difficult and long road ahead of them, and several rural folks feel left out (Catte, 2017; Cramer, 2016; Wuthnow, 2018) Having experienced most of my career in rural areas, I believe those feelings are to be honored. We need to understand why rural Americans fly the flag of rebellion, continue to support Trump after almost 800,000 Americans died from COVID-19, as of January 1, 2022, and why rural Americans feel as if their voice does not matter.

OUTLINE OF THE BOOK

In these next chapters I hope you will find some starting places for dialogue and conversation. The book's next chapters examine rural education utilizing New York's rural schools as a starting point for answering Thier et al.'s (2021) call for more research in the northeastern region. Chapter 1 examines the problem definition of rural educational realities in New York State. The chapter's frame is Kingdon's (2011) agenda setting theory which identifies how a problem rises to the level of a policy discussion for consideration and possible implementation. The chapter explains the different parts of agenda-setting theory, and then, using New York's rural schools, describes examples of different ways that the theory is applicable to the local, New York-based rural districts.

Chapter 2 provides a case study of a failed school district consolidation in New York State. Amid economic hardship, the community of Herkimer, New York, decided to forgo the financial incentives of consolidation, and remain alone. The chapter gives the history and the process about consolidation and reorganization for school districts in New York State. The chapter is one of the first to utilize online posts as a source describing the general points made by opposition groups to school consolidation, when normally these discussions are informal and tend to "vanish" unless someone is at the table. Chapter 2 identifies specifically the overall general points of opposition to consolidation and questions the overall narrative from research and mainstream media which focus on identity loss as a specific reason behind defeating consolidation (Jakubowski, 2019).

Chapter 3 is another example case study (Stake, 1995), from my dissertation (Jakubowski, 2019) which examines a second unsuccessful consolidation in New York State. In this chapter, I examine the reasons two small rural communities, experiencing economic and demographic decline, and the fiscal impact of the Great Recession (Sipple and Yao, 2015) adding to an already economically difficult situation, was unable to access the state Reorganization aid, with one community defeating the consolidation. This is a unique case study, as both communities had previously attempted consolidation with neighboring districts and are regionally close to a successful consolidation which was within the first half decade of completion.

Chapter 4 takes an in-depth examination of New York State's political and educational leadership's continued calls for school district consolidation. The division between pre 2000 and post 2000 traces how the policy in New York became ingrained, and then how leadership continued to repeat the calls as the Great Recession and the aftermath impacted New York State's ability to provide educational support to the most dependent districts in the state. The chapter also examines how rural schools have reacted to loss of state aid, and creatively attempted to ensure their students have access to as many educational and extracurricular activities as possible. The chapter ends with an examination of what possibly is next for school districts.

Chapter 5 explores in depth some of the problems and possibilities facing rural New York schools, as the continued metro centric and urban normative consolidation policy continues to disadvantage rural communities. The chapter provides a roadmap for understanding challenges which rural New York schools continue to face, and how school consolidation is not the answer. The chapter calls for a reassessment of the policy, and an enactment of a different focus for the administration and legislative agendas in the state. A case example of a very recent failed consolidation attempt in Central/Leatherstocking is presented.

Chapter 6 examines the impact on communities of New York when a school is lost after a consolidation. The case studies in the chapter reveal, reinforce, and communicate how rural New York communities which were promised a successful consolidation would help their communities instead experienced what Lyson (2002); Miller, 2021; Schafft (2016); and Sipple et al. (2019) describe as a decline in the community vacated by the building closure.

Chapter 7 explores the question of "Is New York Unique?" In examining the state, despite the large numbers of research and practitioner universities and colleges, and a number of research centers, I argue that New York can be a role model for other states who are urban normative and metro centric.

Chapter 8, the conclusion, captures summary areas of discussion concerning rural education in metro centric, urban normative states. The chapter creates a focus for future research and describes ways that we can alter the current deficit and decline narrative to one of celebration.

Chapter 1

Problem Definition in Rural New York

Since 2010, following the Great Recession (Sipple and Yao, 2015) and increased national educational performance accountability (Cervone, 2017; Schneider and Gottlieb, 2021), New York State government has implemented increased levels of programmatic and fiscal accountability on local school districts. This action by the state, coupled with decreasing revenues for school operations, has led to a renewed interest in changing local school district governance through consolidation (Gormley, 2013; King, 2012). New York State government officials have publicly pushed for consolidating school districts. The pressure to consolidate districts is especially evident in smaller rural communities (Howley and Howley, 2006; Parkerson and Parkerson, 2015). For many rural communities in New York State, an inability to provide, according to the State, an acceptable level of education to their students has been identified as a problem. Adequate education has been defined as growth or achievement on state assessments as defined by "Adequate Yearly Progress" or "AYP" by No Child Left Behind and other federal measures, such as Race to the Top, and Every Student Succeeds Act (Hess and Eden, 2021). There is debate about what the provision of an adequate education means. State officials have identified rural schools as deficient in meeting the educational needs of their citizens (Gormely, 2013; King, 2012; Lundine, 2008; Suozzi, 2008). At the local level, schools do not perceive their provision of education as the problem. Rather it is the perceived State's inability to provide adequate resources that is viewed as the real issue in the local school's ability to provide adequate education (NYSSBA, 2013).

Researchers in education need a clear definition of the problems facing rural schools. Using Kingdon's (2011) Multiple Streams Model of agenda setting as a framework, the problem definition becomes clearer to the researcher. The parts of Kingdon's problem definition allow for a rigorous examination and definition of the problem facing local school boards: how to provide an adequate education for their students in a rural context which will meet the stated goal of a "21st century college and career ready student" (New York State Board of Regents).

DEFINITIONS

A word about language is for this chapter. There are multiple definitions of rural, and this paper will use the National Clearing House for Educational Statistics (NCES, 2022). NCES (2011/2022) Defines rural schools as:

> Rural: Fringe: Census-defined rural territory that is less than or equal to 5 miles from an urbanized area, as well as rural territory that is less than or equal to 2.5 miles from an urban cluster.
>
> Distant: Census-defined rural territory that is more than 5 miles but less than or equal to 25 miles from an urbanized area, as well as rural territory that is more than 2.5 miles but less than or equal to 10 miles from an urban cluster.
>
> Remote: Census-defined rural territory that is more than 25 miles from an urbanized area and is also more than 10 miles from an urban cluster.

According to the New York State Education Department, the major form of school governance reform is called "reorganization" (Chabe, 2011). This term has multiple layers of meaning and can confuse the actual discussion. Schools reorganize frequently, at yearly board of education meetings at the local level, and other less startling events (McDermott, 1999; Tracy, 2010). A more precise term is "consolidation." The consolidation of a school district occurs when the existing district is disincorporated and combined with a neighboring school district. A new, legal, taxing, and governing authority is then created (Brasington, 1999; Chabe, 2011). A third term may be used, "merged" but carries pejorative connotations used in the media and in personal dialogue (Theobald, 1997). When not directly quoting a source, the term consolidation will be utilized. This chapter examines problem definition by school boards which will lead to discussions on consolidation.

This chapter is unique in its application of Kingdon's (2011) Multiple Streams Model to local school boards discussing rural school consolidation on their institutional agenda. To be sure, a review of the literature has found several research studies (Fairman and Donis-Keller, 2012; Galway et al., 2013; Lucas, 2013; Wallin, 2007; Wallner, 2014) which have applied Kingdon's methods to state level agenda setting for rural school consolidation. But that research specifically examines the creation of a policy window and how the Kingdon model can be applied to the state level of agenda setting (Liu et al., 2010). Most research studies use the Kingdon model for agenda setting at the national and state level (Jones et al., 2015; Young et al., 2010). In that research, Kingdon's Policy Window receives a significant amount of attention by researchers (McLendon and Cohen-Vogel, 2008). Yet it is also important to view *local* agenda setting as significant due to the level of control local school boards have in determining education conditions in terms of the selection of the superintendent, setting the local tax levy (constrained by state law) and balancing the limited resources with the unlimited wants and needs of the community (Fischel, 2010).

This chapter, in the first section, reviews four types of agenda setting research. The second section then defines the Kingdon (2011) Multiple Stream model of agenda setting. The third section explains why Kingdon's (2011) model can be applied to the problems faced by rural districts in providing educational services to their population. The fourth section identifies how the problem stream at the local level has moved beyond the rhetoric of rural schools' failure to provide students with an education which prepares them for the twenty-first century. The fourth section systematically reviews the four major parts of Kingdon's problem stream: indicators, focusing events, feedback, and comparisons, discussed at the local educational decision-making level. The final section discusses the critiques of the Kingdon Model and draws conclusions about the agenda setting model as applied to the local level.

AGENDA SETTING RESEARCH

Political scientists research how a problem becomes part of the formal, institutional agenda by describing different theories of agenda setting. The research falls into four major categories of agenda setting: Phase model, Streams model, Diffusion Model, and Rounds Model. Each of the four identified models examines the role of policy actors in identifying a problem, the creation of an event that focuses attention on a problem, and the creation of a solution (Birkland, 2001; Teisman, 2000). Each of the four models will be examined briefly, specifically using the researcher most closely identified with that model as the accepted definition.

The Phase Model of research (Cobb and Elder, 1983) explains how agendas are set by three competing parts: the conflict between groups over resources; the competition between elite and mass decision makers; and the types of groups that are mobilized to successfully address an issue on the agenda. The agenda is set in distinct phases, which occur in a logical and predictable order. Cobb and Elder (1983) describe the reasons people become involved in solving conflict as part of four groups:

1. Manufactured by one group that perceives bias (readjusters)
2. Exploiters—raise issue for personal gains
3. Unanticipated events—circumstantial reactors
4. Do gooders, who wish to help others. (p. 82)

The authors further define two groups in competition for leadership in solving the agenda issue: the elites and the mass decision makers. The elites are the elected or appointed members within a community that have formal power to influence the decision-making process through their connections and control. They have power, which is defined as the ability to make or prevent an event from occurring. The elites are counterbalanced by the mass decision makers, who propose that problems and the solutions should be decided by the widest membership in the community. The mass decision makers will attempt to bring the greatest number of people into the decision-making process using media, personal appeals, and portraying the elites as stealing power through unfair power grabs that disenfranchise decision makers (Cobb and Elder, 1983, p. 43).

When the public becomes involved in the agenda setting process, they are part of one of four groups:

1. Identification Groups: affiliate with the problem
2. Attention Groups: certain specific issues raise their concern
3. Mass Public: public attentive, who are general informed and interested
4. General Public: less active, interested and informed. (Cobb and Elder, 1983, pp. 105–8)

The elites and the mass decision makers compete to influence the groups that will help decide the implementation of the selected and chosen strategy for solving the problem on the agenda. Once the agenda contains their problem, then a potential solution, which the influencer proposes, can see the light of day.

A second research tradition within this field is the "Punctuated Equilibrium" theory. Baumgartner and Jones (1993) argue that most policy making processes are stagnant, with small, hurried intervals that push agenda setting and action during a reaction to a crisis. Agenda setting is still in phases, but now relies on a crisis and a reaction to a crisis in order to move the problem along the agenda setting process. The second model or Multiple Streams Model will be dealt with in more detail in the section below.

The third model, the Diffusion Model (Berry and Berry, 1990), describes an agenda setting process that begins in one location and diffuses to other agenda setting bodies. This model ascribes the agenda setting process to decision makers needing to appear in action as they react to a condition or perceived condition. The diffusion model of agenda setting research postulates communication and feedback loops between neighboring decision makers allowing the idea to spread. The media receives a significant amount of credit in the research literature for spreading the agenda problems across borders. The diffusion model demonstrates how ideas can spread between locations as research is conducted, decision makers share ideas, and problems emerge in multiple locations.

The Rounds Model, the fourth model, is also referred to as the cyclical model. The rounds model examines decision making from the actor within the agenda setting process. As actors move in and out of the agenda setting process, and decisions are made, the actions that have been taken are considered much more in-depth than in the other models presented (Teisman, 2000). Within this model, the researchers attempt to establish a chain of events that leads to the agenda setting and decision-making process.

The Multiple Streams Model provides an adequate vehicle for addressing the problem rural communities face when providing education to their students. The Cobb and Elder (1983), and Baumgartner and Jones (1993) models describe a systematic, linear approach that may not capture the messiness of local decision making. The diffusion model, while having some merit, does not adequately address the control local boards of education have in their local communities. Rural school boards do communicate with each other, but the decision making is local. The Rounds model holds promise in that it describes an iterative approach to decision making but does not allow researchers to clearly distinguish the problem definition that is inherent in most rural communities.

DEFINING KINGDON'S MODEL

Kingdon's Multiple Streams Model of agenda setting (2011) contains three major components: the three streams of agenda setting, the "policy window" and the policy entrepreneur who merges the three streams of agenda setting to create the policy window. These three subsections work in concert to move a problem onto a governing body's agenda for active consideration. According to Kingdon (2011), a problem will be left off the agenda if the three major subcomponents do not exist in a way that catches the attention of the decision-making body.

Kingdon defines the three streams as parallel activities that are divided up into separate parts. They are the problem, the policy, and the politics stream (Kingdon, 2011, p. 87). The problem stream, the focus of this paper, is the movement of a condition, which exists, and there is no government solution, to a problem, which is something the government can work on to solve. In the next section of the paper, the problem stream will be defined in greater detail. The policy stream is the existence of potential policy solutions that may exist in order to solve a problem. These potential policy solutions are theoretical and exist in the "primordial policy soup" until they are "coupled" with the problem and political stream. The third stream, the political stream, is the methods, people, and existing conditions that surround the community in which the decision-making agenda is set. If the problem stream is the "what," then the policy stream is the "how" and the political stream is the "who" of an agenda.

None of the three streams can merge without a "policy entrepreneur" (Kingdon, 2011, p. 181) who is an advocate for a specific policy that can solve the potential problem which exists in the political milieu of the community. The policy entrepreneur has the means, as well as the networking ability, to convince the decision-making body of the necessity of dealing with a problem on their agenda. This person may be formally part of the government in a leadership position, or exist outside of the formal government structure, but hold sway with interest groups who attempt to influence the decision-making governing body. Typically, a policy entrepreneur will attempt to define the problem so that control of the policy solution is theirs as well. When the three streams of agenda setting merge, with a policy entrepreneur's help, a "policy window" is created. The policy window is the "opportunity for advocates to push for their solutions . . . or to focus on their special problems" (Kingdon, 2011, p. 165). The problem is placed on the decision-making agenda, the formal list of problems a decision-making body is addressing at that moment. In Kingdon's (2011) theory, a special event, or a "focusing event" (p. 96) may be required to thrust the problem into the spotlight, and call people's attention to the need to address the problem, with that potential policy solution, in that exact political climate. When the window closes, the decision-making body has moved beyond that problem, and it no longer exists on the formal agenda. The problem may re-emerge, but the three parts of the model must, in Kingdon's model, reconvene. The policy entrepreneur carries the problem and solution on, waiting for another opportunity to re-open the policy window and re-merge the three separate streams.

SELECTING KINGDON AND THE PROBLEM

Kingdon's model has been selected for three specific reasons. First, Kingdon provides a clear framework for defining the problem perceived by state and local leadership about education in rural schools. Second, Kingdon's model has, as far as research permits, been applied to rural, local, educational decision makers in the United States, not to mention and specifically in New York State. Third, the Multiple Streams Agenda setting model explains the process of institutional agenda setting in a structured and organized manner that moves beyond the rhetoric which has emerged on the issue. The common public good of schooling rhetoric has focused on rural schools as expensive remnants of a bygone era in New York (Corbett, 2015; Pugh, 1994; Rassmussen, 2009). The Multiple Streams Model enlightens the reality of problem definition within the communities that face pressure at the state level to consolidate.

Identifying the education problem has two specific aspects. First, rural school research has received increased attention in some areas of research in the area of educational administration. Three studies have discussed the specific circumstances of rural schools in New York State. Macan (2012); Steele (2010), and Tangorra (2013), examine rural districts and the challenges they face. Steele (2010) and Tangorra (2013), specifically, explore the impact of school consolidation in communities. At the national level, researchers based out of Cornell University (Casto et al., 2016; Sipple et al., 2004) have examined the interconnectedness of New York schools and the relationship to their host communities. Two researchers (Henig, 2009; McHenry-Sorber, 2009), have published on the role of state governors pushing for school consolidation. What one piece missing from the research is the agenda setting by the local school boards, as the researchers cited in this paragraph are from the sociological or educational research traditions and are not focused on the local political implications.

The second reason for selecting the problem is a personal one (Ellis et al., 2011). My first teaching job was in a rural school during the process of a consolidation decision. Utilizing recent discussions about the application of personal experience to research, the chapter describes events which have influenced my academic career (White and Corbett, 2014). Autoethnography is a powerful theory paradigm, which combines researcher's personal experience with a desire to seek historical roots of events which they experience.

In 1998, the Cattaraugus and Little Valley Central School District Boards of Education had scheduled a vote to consider the annexation of Little Valley CSD into Cattaraugus CSD. This consolidation is called for in the 1958 Master Plan for School reorganization (NYSED, 1958), the guiding policy document for school reorganization in New York State. Little Valley residents voted to support the merger, but Cattaraugus defeated the proposal by almost 200 votes (Snyder, 1998). This was not the first time in the forty-year history (to that point) that a reorganization vote had failed (Jakubowski, 2020a). Later, in 2002, the author was again affected, as an immediate family member was terminated from employment when the school district downsized the teaching staff after consolidating (Unadilla Valley, 2013). The contract held a no-layoff provision valid for five years. The budget issues sparked my desire to explore rural school consolidation in New York State in an academic fashion (Jakubowski, 2004; Jakubowski, 2013; Jakubowski, 2014; Jakubowski, 2014b; Jakubowski, 2014c; Jakubowski, 2014d; Jakubowski, 2019; Jakubowski, 2020a; Jakubowski, 2021). Specifically, some of my research questions asked why district residents supported or opposed consolidations, especially considering the increased state fiscal aid for successful consolidation. The money the state offered seemed needed to local districts during times of economic downturn. The research thread I undertook mirrors international trends in the development of sound practices as people combine personal experiences in academic pursuits (Corbett, 2021; Schulte and Walker-Gibbons, 2016; White and Corbett, 2014).

A debate within the research questions the effectiveness of consolidations. Duncombe and Yinger (2007), examining New York State schools found that consolidations do not inherently save money. Savings occurred with very small district consolidations. Usually, the total populations of the combined districts should be less than 1000 students. Since saving money is one of the main points the state officials use to support consolidation, this research raises questions about the validity of the second claim, improved educational opportunities for students.

A second study by Nitta et al. (2010) found some improvement in educational opportunities in their single case study. Since increased academic offerings is a second reason for proposing a school district consolidation, the question is what types of educational offerings are usually found after consolidation.

The two most frequent reasons for consolidation, efficiency, and effectiveness in educational programming have been offered as the "official narrative" rationale for undertaking school reorganization studies at the local level (Jakubowski, 2019).

DEFINING THE PROBLEM

Kingdon (2011) demonstrates that problems are composed of a variety of subparts that influence decision maker's choices to include issues on their active agenda. His framework establishes indicators, focusing events/crises/symbols, feedback, and comparisons as the sub parts of a problem. In his original model, Kingdon considers the case of a budget as a problem indicator. A budget referendum defeat may be classified as a focusing event as well. Within the last five years, education in rural communities has seen an upswing in attacks on its efficiency and provision of programming for students (Flora, Flora, and Gasteyer, 2016; Howley and Howley, 2015). Kingdon, and other researchers in the area of agenda setting agree that a negative situation within a community, called a condition, creates anxiety and discussion, but does not rise to the level of a problem, which is defined as a condition that government intervention will improve. For rural communities within New York State, the school boards, the professional administrators, and to some extent, members of the community have defined the declining performance of their schools as a problem that should be dealt with by the locally elected board of education. Community residents are dissatisfied with a perceived shortcoming of their school. For some residents who are graduates of the district, they believe their personal education experience is superior to the one their children are receiving. For other members of the community who chose to move into the area, the schools were an attraction, and they have become disappointed with the results and the observed decline in the school program. The community members are examining the four parts of the problem stream, and in conjunction with their locally elected school boards are beginning to discuss alternatives to the status quo. The problem stream of Kingdon's model contains indicators, focusing events/crises/symbols, feedback and comparisons in order to establish a problem that the local board of education will need to consider on its formal, institutional agenda. This paper will specifically explore the four parts of the problem stream in Kingdon's model and classify source material using this paradigm.

Education provision by rural schools in New York has been identified as a concern by the governor, the former commissioner of education, and local school boards. Within the rural communities, where this paper focuses, local school leadership finds they can no longer educate children to the level the community expects. The boards of education define the problem as a decrease in the level of education provided to students, and increased expectations from parents, the state, and local businesses.

INDICATORS

The first part of the problem stream is indicators. Indicators are information, data, and other reported statistics that indicate the existence of a problem. Indicators can help decision makers in examining a problem by revealing the magnitude or change in the status of the problem (Kingdon, 2011, p. 91). Indicators are combined into reports that are then interpreted by decision makers to reveal the extent of a problem within a governmental jurisdiction. In rural schools, indicators have been gathered through multiple sources.

One primary example of indicators for rural schools is the annual state test results. These test results emerge from standardized assessments administered to all children in a public school for grades 3–8 in English Language Arts and math (NYSED, 2014). Other standardized exams include the fourth grade and eighth grade science, and the Regents exams in high school for eleventh grade English Language Arts, math (grade nine), science (grade nine), and social studies in tenth and eleventh grade. Once the exams have been graded and normed, the results are released to the public and local media outlets by the State Education Department. In the two districts selected for a pilot study (Jakubowski, 2014a) the test results for the elementary (3–8) performance indicators saw a decline. This decline was especially pronounced in the students with disabilities subpopulation. This achievement/accountability data is used by SED to determine if the school is in good standing and can continue to receive federal aid without improvement actions, or the school is in accountability and requires intervention by the state education department (Jimerson, 2005).

A second indicator schools utilize is demographic information contained on the official New York State Education Department's report card (Azano et al., 2020). Local school districts, at the behest of state and federal agencies, collect a significant amount of demographic data that is utilized in policy, funding, and accountability decision making. The district collects in a yearly census the population of school-aged children within the district. In many rural communities in New York, including those in pre-dissertation and dissertation research (Jakubowski, 2019), school-aged student population is flat or declining. Mirroring national research, many areas of white dominate communities are facing similar demographic trends The census information is used to help determine staff sizes, classroom sizes, building utilization, as well as applying for state and federal grants. This data on population is coupled with information on student mobility. Districts need to account for students who move out of and into their districts. In many rural districts, including the two that were examined in the pilot study, high rates of student mobility are apparent (Jakubowski, 2014b; Schafft, 2006). Additional data is collected on the socio-economic status of its families through two sources. The first source collected yearly is the free and reduced lunch application. This information allows the school to plan for the number of students who will receive federally and state subsidized breakfasts and lunches. This information assists districts in confirming data collected from the second source, the federal census on poverty. This information also determines how much federal aid in the form of Title I poverty aid the district is entitled to. The information paints a picture of how poor the district is becoming, as the district will experience an increase in the free and reduced lunch count before the federal census on poverty begins to indicate an issue (Azano et al., 2020).

The second indicator districts gather is graduation rate. This data has two-fold purposes. First, it is used as a local effectiveness measure by the community. Second, the state utilizes the data as an accountability measure for student performance. This data, like the testing data, is used to judge a school and determine if it is "in good standing" or "in accountability status." The residents join in celebrating the achievement of their students in the conclusion of their high school careers. For many members of the community, graduation marks the transition into the workforce. For others, it symbolizes leaving the community for college, and a career away from their hometown. As Corbett (2007); Corbett (2015); Carr and Kefelas (2009); Sherman and Sage (2011); Sherman (2021); and Smarsh (2018) as well as others have found, many rural students leave their local communities to search for career opportunities that are not available in their hometowns. The graduates seek entry into a labor market that is not locally based, but globally based. Carr and Kefelas (2009); Corbett (2007); Schafft and Jackson (2010); Theobald and Alsmeyer (1995), and others have found that schools in rural communities are torn between preparing students for "place based" opportunities and preparing students to compete in a global environment. Their research has found rural schools are contributing to their own demise, as many graduates are prepared for careers and education that is not relevant to the local environment.

A third indicator used by schools to diagnose their health is teacher recruitment and teacher turnover. Multiple research studies, stretching back for almost 100 years have argued rural schools are disadvantaged in their ability to recruit and retain highly educated and qualified candidates for teaching positions. Some recent research (Miller, 2012; Reagan et al., 2019; See et al., 2020; Tran et al., 2020) has found that rural schools are competing against local suburban districts for teacher education candidates. These suburban communities can offer higher starting pay to teachers, increased specialization within teaching loads, and offer additional remuneration above the pay scales many rural schools can offer. Additionally, suburban districts offer living amenities that most rural areas do not have, such as shopping choices, entertainment options, and a similar age demographic pool for socialization. Other studies have found teacher candidates find living in rural communities difficult. These studies found teachers in rural community's surrender anonymity that urban and suburban teachers can assume in their personal lives. Further, the studies (Eppley, 2015; Schulte and Walker-Gibbs, 2016) have indicated the close-knit aspect of the community can work against teachers who are learning the "ropes alone," especially if they are an outsider recruited into the community. As the teachers gain professional experience, their career options are limited in rural communities, and their pay scales do not keep pace with their cohorts from college. Mid-career teachers begin to explore professional opportunities in suburban areas and may seek to professionally relocate for additional educational and professional opportunities. Additionally, suburban school districts tend to hire teachers with experience into their staff ranks, so many rural schools are considered "training grounds" for new teachers directly from college education schools (Maranto and Schuls, 2012). A recent search revealed that rural teacher morale is not a recent problem, but rather was the subject of study in the mid-twentieth century (Ross, 1960).

Closely associated with teacher recruitment and tenure is administrative recruitment and turnover in a rural district. Recruiting administrators and retaining them within rural districts is a struggle that has been recognized across research on rural schools. This paper will specifically limit its discussion to superintendents for simplicity, but research on principal recruitment and retention has been thoroughly addressed in multiple studies (McHenry-Sorber and Sutherland, 2020). In New York State, the chief executive officer of a local school district is the superintendent. They are selected by an elected board of education that offers an employment contract of between three and five years. In some contracts, the board places a residency requirement, with a stipulation that the purchase or long-term leased residence must be within the district's boundary. Their children are always expected to enroll into the local school. Superintendents serve at the pleasure of boards of education and are asked to serve as the intermediary between the boards and the professional staff of the school district. Superintendents in rural districts have reported in research that their profession is a stressful one and involves frequent nights and weekends (Arnold et al., 2005; Sperry and Hill, 2015).

Additionally, superintendents in rural schools are asked to assume additional administrative responsibilities that are often delegated in suburban or urban districts. These roles may include business manager, spokesperson, teacher evaluator, student discipline arbitrator, special education service coordinator, and a curriculum leader, especially if they serve the dual role as principal. Many superintendents are recruited into rural districts as their first foray into the role, and often seek to move into larger districts. Often, the superintendent is an outsider to the district, and may have few, if any local ties. Frequently, the superintendent is the highest paid person within a community. Research involving superintendents report that many leave their role as superintendent in smaller, rural communities for greater community amenities, additional pay, additional administrative support structure, or a more cooperative board of education. A change in board membership can herald the change in leadership and the district (Arnold et al., 2005; McHenry-Sorber and Sutherland, 2020; Sperry and Hill, 2015).

A sixth indicator of a district's health and performance is the stability of board of education membership. This indicator can be double edged, as a poor board of education can have long standing members who are uninterested in improving the educational program within the community. From another perspective, long standing service on a board can signal interest in learning the nuances of board responsibility and an investment in educational activities by members of a community. If a board of education sees frequent resignation or defeat of members, then the school community or district may be in turmoil (Yarger, 2018). State Education Department monitors board of education election results and will provide technical assistance to superintendents and boards that are in frequent turnover (Tieken, 2014).

A final indicator of district health is the school's budget. There are two parts to this indicator. First, a "fund balance" is the amount of money held in reserve by a school district each year. It is considered a "rainy day fund" for emergency situations. The second part of the indicator is the community's approval of the proposed budget in a yearly referendum. If a school district begins to experience a crisis, the budget will lose its yearly cushion, as the superintendent and the board of education will try and curtail programming reduction and tax increases in order to maintain levels of service to the community and reduce negative taxpayer reaction to an increased tax burden. New York has one of the highest rates of tax burden in the United States. In response to a perception by taxpayers and political leaders that schools were unwisely spending tax revenue from local communities, a two-part policy change was implemented that has negatively affected schools, especially in rural areas. First, the office of state comptroller, in conjunction with the legislature decreased the amount of unreserved fund balance available to a school to 4 percent of the total budget (Yinger, 2020). This action limited the "rainy-day fund" that many rural and small schools depended on in times of economic strain. Second, the legislature, at the governor's urging, implemented a 2 percent limit on the percentage of a tax increase allowed each year. This second action limited the school's ability to raise revenue during times of economic stress (NYSSBA, 2013). A third economic issue emerged during the 2008 economic crash that adversely affected rural schools. In order to preserve state fiscal functioning, a "Gap Elimination Adjustment" was placed on state aid to school districts in the 2010–2011 Executive Budget. The GEA, as it is referred to, reduced the percentage of state aid to local school districts to ensure the state budget stayed solvent. While the GEA did not necessarily reduce state aid absolutely, it did decrease a promised aid increase that many rural districts needed in order to offset increasing poverty and decreasing absolute taxable values in their communities (QUESTAR III, 2010; Yinger, 2020).

These eight indicators as listed above, help to define a condition that is ripe for action by the government in the form of a policy problem. For many leaders in rural communities, the indicators were concerning, but did not necessarily raise alarms. The leadership in rural communities are prepared to "spend both sides of a dollar" (Slentz, 2011). What became more disconcerting was the shift of some of this indicator into serious crises, or a focusing event. This moved the problems of providing a sound education for students onto an agenda for discussion at the local level.

FOCUSING EVENTS/CRISES/SYMBOL

A condition in the local community may not move onto the local decision-making agenda until a significant event, occurrence or a symbol emerges to draw people's attention, both within and beyond an institution to that problem (Kingdon, 2011, p. 94). For some rural schools, a major focusing event could be a serious issue, or to an outsider, a trivial occurrence that shakes the community to the core.

For one school district in New York State, the focusing event which began the consolidation discussion was their football team forfeiting a season. The team was not bad; it did not have enough players to meet state requirements. Only three years earlier, the same team had won the state championship for its size group. To the local community, and to the school, the inability to field a football team was a serious blow to community pride, and serious discussion was needed to remedy the situation.

In a second school district, the school budget was defeated twice in one year. The budget was presented to the local school community with a realization that the school district would need to eliminate several extracurricular activities, cut full day kindergarten to half day, and eliminate all non-essential bussing. Further, the budget proposed a double-digit tax increase. This was well above the 2 percent tax cap allowed by state law. In order to pass such a budget, a supermajority of 60 percent of voters would need to give their positive approval. The budget was soundly defeated, and the school district proposed a second budget. The second budget cut even more from the original proposal, including a librarian, all sports below the varsity level, and all after school bussing except for once a week. The revised budget was again defeated. The school board and superintendent began to explore consolidation with neighboring schools to "save our schools . . . we are approaching educational bankruptcy" (Michael, 2012; Weeks et al., 2002).

Stone (1989) discusses the role of personal stories in creating symbols in crisis moments that can be used to promote policy agenda setting. In one rural district in western New York, the story of the valedictorian of the local community became the symbol for rural school struggles and the need to discuss consolidation (Dzikowski, 2012). When the superintendent testified before the Governor's Commission on Education Reform that the valedictorian of a local school district was "denied admission to SUNY Geneseo because the student's high school preparation didn't have the depth and breadth other schools in the state provide to their students." The valedictorian's story became the focusing story for the plight of rural schools. Hibbard (2012), while interviewing the president of the Yates County, New York chamber of commerce, asked about school aid, and the president of the chamber relayed the story of the valedictorian denied admissions to SUNY Geneseo. Then, in 2014, the *Watertown Daily Times*, in an editorial discussing a potential school consolidation, claimed the Valedictorian as one of St. Lawrence County's own. "Sometime within the last few years, SUNY Geneseo denied admission to a high school valedictorian from St. Lawrence County." The valedictorian as the face of the rural education crisis spread from the Finger Lakes region to the North Country. As more schools in rural communities worried about their valedictorian's chances at selective state schools, other superintendents began to worry about students graduating. Some of the most strident calls for consolidation emerged as superintendents told media and state panels that their schools were months away from an inability to offer state mandated classes (Dawson, 2015; Grant, 2013). This crisis, as well as the symbol of the valedictorian denied admissions to SUNY Geneseo moved consolidation discussion onto the agendas of some school district's boards of education. In many rural communities, the boards received additional information in the form of feedback. We now turn our attention to feedback creating problem stream definition.

FEEDBACK

Feedback is the process of monitoring indicators, receiving complaints, and implementing programs (Kingdon, 2011, p. 100). Local school boards of education receive feedback from three sources that have helped define the problem stream of decreased school performance. The local community membership, local medial, and the state government provide constant feedback to the schools in a variety of ways which result in frequent discussion concerning the school's efforts to fulfill its mission.

Local community members in rural areas are more closely involved with the school than in urban or suburban districts. The school's athletic teams and extracurricular activities provide the only form of community-based entertainment in many small towns. The residents of the schools use its auditorium for political meetings, its gym for scouting meetings, and its classrooms for adult education and extension opportunities. Following the *New Milford* ruling, the school building may host religious services as well (Alexander and Alexander, 2011). Community members may socialize with the principal and superintendent of the district at chamber of commerce meetings, community service events, and shop in the same grocery store as resident teachers in the area. These leaders are often part of community and network building in the hopes of solving cross agency issues (Zuckerman, 2019). Research studies, as cited above, have indicated teachers and administrators are frequently engaged in school related discussions in the store, and while their children are at games and meetings for recreational activities (Zuckerman, 2020). With the superintendent and board of education member's addresses and phone numbers matters of public record, some survey results have reported receiving at-home visits from concerned members of the public and frequent telephone calls at home concerning school issues. Community members feel as taxpayers who have an intimate connection with the local school leaders through professional, social, and proximal associations they can provide their opinion on a wide variety of issues. Further, school board meetings provide members of the public with an opportunity to address the board at their meetings. Members of the public use their same feelings of association to provide the members of the board with feedback on a variety of issues concerning the school. If a community member feels their opinion has not been received through less formal means, they may use letters to the editor of the local newspaper as another route to provide feedback. In the era of social media, members of the community are turning to the internet, specifically Facebook and Twitter to share their opinions about the school district through the formal district websites and on other anonymous web pages that collect opinions about events in the local community (Jakubowski, 2019; Lawson et al., 2017)

The second group locally that provides feedback to the school is the media. The media provides a conduit between the local school and the community through its coverage of school-based events and activities. In rural communities, the school may provide a significant amount of material for the local news media to cover in the form of sports, after school events, the school menu and board of education meetings. The local newspaper will frequently interview the superintendent and principal on a range of issues and may provide elected members or professional members of the school with space to write a weekly column. Administrative staffing issues at the local school district provide interest to the local community, as the superintendent and principal of the school are often high-profile civic leaders, along with the mayor, police chief, fire chief, and religious leaders. Local school children and teachers provide human interest stories to the media, with residents enjoying the keepsake when their children appear in the sports page or award article (Theobald and Wood, 2010).

A newspaper, through its editorial staff, or editor, will write their opinion about the status of the school in editorials or opinion columns. These thought pieces are often widely read by members of the community and form the basis of discussions at the local diner (Cramer, 2016; Schmuck and Schmuck, 1992). The newspapers, in the digital age, provide online comment forums that give readers an opportunity to engage in discussions about materials that have appeared online and in print. This new form of engagement and feedback encouraged by the media has opened a whole new avenue for citizens to provide their local school board feedback.

The third group providing the local school board feedback is the state government. The state government provides feedback to local schools in the form of communication from the Office of the State Comptroller (OSC) and the State Education Department (NYSED). Following the superintendent's theft of public funds from one of the school districts in New York State, and the resulting scandal of the 1990s, the OSC has implemented more stringent auditing procedures and events for local school districts (NYSOSC, 2009). The OSC, on a risk assessment basis, conducts a wide variety of audits in different areas of local school business management. The results of these audits are then published by OSC, and usually involve findings and recommendations for improvement that the schools must address through a corrective action plan submitted to OSC and monitored by the OSC and the New York State Education Department.

In addition to the fiscal monitoring by NYSED, staff will monitor or review local school program implementation. This communication can occur in two ways. First, the department may engage the district in a programmatic review of the school by a member of the Office of Accountability (OA) or by the Special Education Quality Assurance (SEQA) office. Both types of programmatic reviews is time intensive and result in a report detailing the shortcomings of the school that then must be addressed in a corrective action plan. Districts are expected to submit a series of documents to the department for review. These documents can detail fiscal and programmatic activities for federal grants. In more in-depth reviews, a member or team from the State Education Department will spend up to four days physically present in a district. During the review, the staff members will visit classrooms, interview student, parents, teachers, and administrators. They will observe grade level meetings or staff meetings. The district, if it is in Federal Title I poverty alleviation accountability or Special Education Accountability is required by law to submit a detailed corrective action plan yearly to the department for review and comment for revisions. This plan not only requests federal grant expenditure plans, but requests state aid expenditure plans, and local tax revenue expenditure plans (Jakubowski, 2021; Prestipino, 2020; Zuckerman et al., 2018).

The second way NYSED communicates with a local district is through the Board of Cooperative Education Services District Superintendent (DS). A holdover from the earliest days of schools within New York, the DS acts as the field representative of the NYSED to the local school districts in the state (Kachris, 1987). The DS is mandated by the commissioner, the regulations of the State Education Department, and by State Education Law to meet with local school superintendents and discuss the educational program of the local school district. The BOCES DS may provide schools with additional technical assistance and feedback in the form of provider networks (Prestipino, 2020). Usually, most rural districts in New York State were identified for difficulties in meeting special education student performance levels. Previously, many rural schools received assistance from special education providers (RSE-TASC). These centers work directly with schools on a Quality Improvement Plan (QIP) that is a direct result of the special education department's review of the district. For a small district with one superintendent and one principal, a significant amount of time is devoted to meeting the state reporting requirements. Rural school administrators have reported the amount of time they spend in dealing with state education department feedback and requests for additional information have tripled and are an undue burden that removes them from work with the teachers and curriculum efforts (Arnold et al., 2005; Sperry and Hill, 2015; Zuckerman et al., 2018).

COMPARISONS

Problems may be defined by differences between two populations. A comparison allows residents both within, and administrators beyond communities to evaluate levels of achievement between two groups (Kingdon, 2011, p. 111). Residents compare the achievement of their schools against neighboring schools. Sporting events allow people to see the athletic performance of their teams, but the school facilities as well. The State provides a wide variety of public information that the media and citizens use to compare schools. Rural leaders meet in regional meetings and compare experiences.

With a wide range of information readily obtainable in the area of academic performance, tax assessment rates, co-and extracurricular offerings, community members can compare their schools with neighboring districts. Student achievement data from state testing is found in the yearly report card, along with graduation rate data. The report cards include information on teacher experience, certification, and demographic data, all information classified as "indicator information" in Kingdon's (2011) model. Typically, regional media will take this information and create charts that compare school performance in their circulation basin. Often, regional media will produce a yearly guide to local school districts that will include a wide range of programmatic information for residents and business consumption. Real estate agents will then utilize this data to assist families moving into the area during home selection processes. In districts considering consolidation, a state mandated report that is produced by outside consultants will include programmatic information comparisons between the two districts, enrollment trends, workforce expenditure information and benchmarking to other similar sized districts across the state (Schneider, 2018).

Rural administrators are often profoundly overworked, compared to their suburban and rural peers. A single superintendent, or potentially a principal as well split duties which are divided by a team in larger districts. With the implementation of teacher professional evaluations, administrators are now faced with significantly more time evaluating and reporting compliance-based plans. The teacher evaluation of this component is a multi-step process that requires at least three hours minimum to meet and observe the teacher for each of the three minimally required observations (nine total hours). Principals or a superintendent is often the liaison with the parent teacher organization, the state offices for at-risk children, and works frequently and closely with the board of education, and other groups within the school. The principal is requested to attend community events, sporting contests, and serve as a member of community organizations. In larger school districts, other administrators can serve as the contact point, and reduce the overall burden that one individual faces. Finally, student discipline in larger schools is often handled by deans of students or assistant principals. The principal is asked to deal with the most difficult issues, but not the routine ones that are dealt with by assistant principals. The frequent need to interact with students during discipline is time consuming and can become extremely stressful (Casto, 2016; Jakubowski, 2021).

Rural teachers often compare their working conditions with suburban and urban counterparts. With the comparisons easily available through the internet, personal connections, and experience, many rural teachers find the comparisons between rural and suburban communities favoring suburban teaching experiences and will leave rural schools for suburban communities (Jakubowski, 2020a; Miller, 2012; Opfer, 2011).

Using data, personal experience, and professional judgment comparing schools, the rural educational leadership may see a condition has developed, which may then morph into a problem that the decision-making body, or school board and professional administrators should solve. The comparisons between rural schools and suburban schools have led some districts, especially in rural areas, to seek a policy solution of improving the comparison their districts receive with other schools through exploring consolidation. To improve their academic, social, and economic attractiveness, the school districts believe that by becoming bigger, more families, teachers, and businesses will seek out their community as a location.

CONCLUSION

The Kingdon (2011) model's application explored within this paper provides a framework for examining problems in a rural community struggling to provide its students with an adequate level of education when faced with declining population, loss of resources, and increased state pressures and mandates. By specifically examining the problem stream of Kingdon's model, the four subparts of problem identification emerge and allow the critical examination of how school communities begin to explore the policy solution of consolidation as a board of education on a formal agenda. By helping us move the debate from the rhetoric to research-based inquiry, the Kingdon model can help clearly identify the problem stream from theoretical to concrete. Further, the Multiple Streams Model of Kingdon enables researchers to explore the agenda setting process that school boards undertake during a highly emotional time period in a school community. When a rural community begins the discussion to end its school's existence, people's passions emerge. Rural communities believe in self-sufficiency, and are leery of governmental intervention (Feldmann, 2003; Rassmussen, 2009).

The Kingdon (2011) Model is not perfect. Researchers have identified areas of the Kingdon model that are questioned. The critiques include a focus on institutions, the lack of rigor in the model, the separations of the model from other traditions, and a downplay of the media's role of agenda setting. Each critique will be briefly examined.

First, the Multiple Streams Model does not allow researchers to predict *"what kinds of problems are likely to be coupled with what kinds of solutions* (italics in original)" (Mucciaroni, 1992, p. 463). The model also takes as givens the institutions and the "rules of the game" that are in operation and does not question the *effect* those rules have on a problem reaching the agenda (Mucciaroni, 1992). Finally, Mucciaroni (1992) critique of the Kingdon model indicates the focus on the policy entrepreneur does not allow enough attention on the role a leader plays within a reform process. He indicates that "the reforms afforded leaders an opportunity to enhance their reputations" (p. 470). By not studying this motivation, the model is lacking depth of analysis.

Second, the critique of Multiple Streams articulated by Cairney and Jones (2015) involves the flexibility of the model. Kingdon's research paradigm is too flexible and does not require a rigid adherence to a defining model with in-depth research. Cairney and Jones further (2015) critique the model for its lack of development. Specifically, they compare multiple streams model with three other agenda setting models and find a lack of theoretical literature that pushes the model and refines it deeper. Specifically, they cite Kingdon's lack of involvement in further researching and adjusting the model.

Third, Howlett et al. (2015), believe that the Multiple Streams Model and the Policy Cycle model should be united to explain the agenda setting process as a reaction to historical events that the Kingdon Model does not consider. In their efforts, a "policy development" stream (p. 426) is added to the streams model and combined with a "programme stream" (p.427) that describes the implementation process and adjustments.

In a review of the historical development of Kingdon's book, Baumgartner (2016), found that Kingdon's sources may have influenced his downplay of the media as an influential agent. By the sources he selected for the interviews, and the data Kingdon received during interviews, the media's influence on the policy process is not rated nearly as influential as Dearing and Rogers (1996), two scholars of media studies found in their research. The role of media as an influencing agent in agenda setting is discussed in Stone, and other researchers.

Further research should explore other parts of the Kingdon (2011) Agenda Setting model in rural educational settings. The policy stream and political stream, as well as the policy entrepreneurs are areas that are rich with materials and should be examined in future research, especially at the local school board level. While the research cited above demonstrates that the Policy Window emerge when a school community is in crisis, there has been little research into the role the policy entrepreneurs play in promoting or mitigating the public perception of crisis. The role the media plays in setting the stage for the policy window opening in a rural community will also require further research. This is especially relevant as the role of media is beginning to shift with the expanding use of the internet as a source of information (Eissler et al., 2014).

The analysis in this chapter is unique in that it is the first time that the Kingdon (2011) Multiple Stream Model of Agenda setting has been applied to local rural boards of education in New York State. This chapter examined agenda setting research by discussing briefly the four research models that are most prevalent. The Kingdon model was described in detail, with the three major subparts examined: the streams, policy window, and policy entrepreneur. This paper then discussed the selection of Kingdon's model and the selection of the educational issue and the rationale behind those decisions. The four parts of the problem stream were discussed in detail, with applications to rural districts highlighted. Kingdon's problem stream suggests the definition of the stream includes indicators, focusing events/symbols, feedback, and comparisons. Finally, the chapter examined conclusions that can be drawn from the research, and the critiques of the model.

Chapter 2

The "Hidden Narrative"

Rural schools are described as the heart and soul of a community. For the past 100+ years, a battle has been fought between advocates for local control and consolidation efforts. One such recent study indicated

> education researchers can respond to this call for resistance by using place inquiry and spatial methods to surface patterns of inequality and oppression *as well as* localized opportunities for people and communities to challenge these patterns in the context of education policy and practice. (Butler and Sinclair, 2020, p. 84)

With decreasing state and local level resources for education, and increasing mandates, many districts are struggling to meet educational programs mandated by policy. State legislative incentives offered by New York promote school reorganization, or consolidation. This case study, part of pre-dissertation (Jakubowski, 2019) research, examines the reasons voters in Herkimer Central School District chose to forgo merger. The case study is an example (Stake, 1995) because the district residents voted twice before to consolidate. This pattern occurs in almost every attempt. Considering the publicly stated position of the former governor of New York's stance that smaller, rural schools should consolidate, the population made an informed decision to reject the merger plan with two other communities that were similar. The community lost an additional 40 percent in operating aid over 14 years in a time when the economy of school operations is tight.

Historically, school improvement policy, or reorganization has an almost 100-year history in the state (Deantoni, 1971; Heffernan, 2021; Monk and Haller, 1986; Pugh, 1994). There exists a significant body of professional and practical research available to practitioners and researchers alike (see Jakubowski, 2019). Media members are very active in reporting the status of local school consolidation discussions. Newspaper and television outlets focus on the role identity and by extension sports play in the consolidation efforts. The research literature is more expansive than just the role of identity. Literature reviews (see Jakubowski, 2019) indicated there are four areas of consolidation discussions: the role of identity, consolidation for program enhancement, consolidation for economic efficiency and state mandates for mergers. Research literature tends to focus on the role of identity and the view that others do not understand the role of the local school within the community (Jakubowski, 2019, Sipple et al., 2019). Seeking to support or refute this analysis, this exemplar case study (Stake, 1995) was undertaken examining the content of on-line discussion board posts focusing on the failure of the Herkimer merger.

In order to see if my experiences in the Cattaraugus-Little Valley merger were unique, or were experienced by wider communities (Ellis et al., 2001), I examined additional reorganization attempts. My theory of action was grounded in Kyvig's (2019) approach of utilizing "nearby history" to gather information. First, I examined newspaper reports, school board minutes. Then, trying to channel the work of Essert and Howard (1952), I wanted to meet people. In order to accomplish this task, I used the internet as an archive. An online participation board, TOPIX, had a wide range of individual posts, responses, and reactions to the reorganization attempt, and allowed me, an outsider, to access thoughts. I utilized the work of Gee (2014) in the form of discourse analysis, which is essentially what historians do through documentary research. These posts were informative, and having been created by people who were witnesses to events, and were not triggered by my questioning, I believe that they most clearly resemble organic reasons to create a narrative (Lowenthal, 1998). Responses which create a false positive to presented researcher interviews or survey questions is a major concern in human subject responses (Rimando et al., 2015). Content analysis of previous materials begins to move into the historical research tradition, which favors the use of documents in the creation of phenomena explanation (Jakubowski, 2019). These online posts are as close to journals, diaries, and what Cramer (2016) did in interviewing people via observation.

I was intrigued to understand if, as most of the research indicated, that identity is a powerful reason for the defeat of a consolidation. According to research, now in rural areas in particular, rural identity leads to specific self descriptions. Rural residents are not urban. They seek to establish their "in group" as different from urban areas, and as Trujillo (2022) points out "rural residents tend to dismiss intellectuals, often associated with cities." With rural communities, residents are often troubled by people who have more status or power, even if that is just a perception. In this particular case study, the identity points were not really about urban versus rural, rather more concerned with different, more practical concerns. In my experiences (Ellis et al., 2011) and confirmed through the examination of events leading up to the reorganization attempt, residents were concerned about the impact, economically, of a four-way centralization. Residents really struggled to understand how, if the State was facing economic difficulties with the Great Recession of 2008, the government could afford to provide significantly higher amounts of incentive aid to school communities.

Five areas emerged from an initial review of the posts:

1. Personal attacks—defined as a post that attacked another poster or person on a personal level
2. Superintendent—a post dealing with the superintendent of the school district
3. Board of Education—a post dealing with the board of education
4. Teachers—posts that deal with some aspect of teachers
5. State—A post with some reference to New York State or a state agency

Within each category, contributors cited economic factors that the school should have addressed internally before moving to the consolidation vote. A recurring theme in these case study discussions revolve around the complexity of public education funding and personal home-based funding. National conversation concerning education has increasingly argued the current model is unsustainable due to the high salaries and benefits package members of the profession receive from public funding. Public rhetoric has claimed that education and government spending is wasteful, and needs oversight, accountability, and budget cuts necessary to reduce taxes.

STATE MERGER PROCESS

Following the consolidation of Brooklyn and Queens into Manhattan, many citizens felt their rights had been ignored by the process, and a constitutional provision was added to ensure that citizens in any municipality facing consolidation would have to approve the vote (Benjamin and Nathan, 2001). State law establishes a thorough process to ensure the rights of citizens within school districts are upheld during the study and voting process. The consolidation process begins with one board of education approaching a contiguous area requesting that the two (or more) groups engage in a feasibility study to determine if reorganization of the districts is a viable option. The two boards then procure an efficiency study from the New York State Department of State (typically around $35,000–45,000) that will be utilized by the districts to hire a consultant firm to undertake the study and write an official report to the State Education Department. This action is recorded in a formal vote by both boards of education. The selection of the consultants is another vote by the boards of education. The districts will then call for several volunteers representing major stakeholders throughout the two or more communities to serve on the task force charged with examining the reorganization process of the school districts. The taskforce committees often number in the teens to twenty members, from both communities engaged in the discussion (Chabe, 2011).

The consultants will then hold, over the span of one to two years, a series of public forums and task force meetings where all facets of the communities and schools are reviewed. Some areas reviewed include, but are not limited to are:

- Administrative structure of the schools, including the number and term of years boards of education serve
- Teaching staff, including assignment and pay and benefits scales
- Support staff, including assignments, pay, benefits scales
- Curriculum offerings at the elementary, middle and secondary levels
- Extracurricular activities offered
- Transportation routes and expenses
- Building utilization and demographic trends for the next ten years
- Tax rates and state aid to school budgets. (Chabe, 2011)

Report findings are presented to the community in intervals, with opportunities for questions at the public forums advertised in print and electronic media. The reports recommend what curriculum enhancements can be expected from the consolidation, where cost savings can be achieved, how buildings can be utilized, and how the additional state aid should be used to lower taxes, "level up" existing contract provisions, and save for future expenses. One interesting note to recognize, before the 2010s, many reports recommended contracts were adjusted in favor of the bargaining units. In the mid to late 2010s, the recommendations included negotiating contracts to ensure the district could reduce expenditures through greater employee share of healthcare. After the report outlining the reorganization is prepared, it is submitted to the state for review and recommendations. Once the department has signed off on the report, the local boards of education are asked to approve the reports and request permission from the State Education Department to hold a non-binding referendum or "straw vote" on the question of reorganization. The straw vote, when held, must pass in both communities. If either community votes the proposal down, the process dies. If the straw vote passes, the question is sent to a binding referendum. Again, in both communities the question must pass for the merger to commence, usually on July 1 immediately following the vote (Chabe, 2011). In an interesting occurrence, approximately 80 percent of straw votes pass in both communities. Almost

90 percent of binding votes fail in at least one of the communities. Some reasons why are discussed later, but often the opposition cite the need for internal spending reduction before a significant change, such as a reorganization happens.

Post 2008: Struggles

In 2008, a combination of major economic difficulties resulted in three major problems in the state of school finance in New York. The Gap Elimination Adjustment, the increase in pension costs, and the 2 percent tax levy cap created a perfect storm of economic issues that have hurt smaller schools. First, the economic declines lead to the suspension of the implementation of the Campaign for Fiscal Equity's state aid increases. The enacted budget imposed a Gap Elimination Adjustment (GEA) to the state aid portion of school budgets. The GEA was designed to help the state close a significant state level budget deficit. In New York, educational spending constitutes close to 50 percent of the states over all spending plans. Proportionately speaking, the GEA affected small, rural districts that are poor to a larger extent than wealthy suburban districts. This is due to the reality the smaller, rural schools are significantly dependent on state aid to offer education to the students within their borders (Sipple and Yao, 2015).

Second, the New York State pension system is tied into the New York City based Stock Market. The state's pension system is supported by a constitutional mandate that the system must be solvent. When employees' contributions and stock performance do not ensure the plan is solvent, employer contributions must increase. In the early 2000s, New York passed legislation allowing contributors who had reached a ten-year milestone to cease contributions to the system. This, along with the loss of stock value, hurt the pension system. Employer contributions have risen from single digit percent of contributions to 37 percent or higher, a figure that has resulted in districts facing the conundrum of cutting today's services to pay for tomorrow's retirees (Sipple and Yao, 2015).

Part of New York Governor Andrew Cuomo's budget in 2012, the state imposed a 2 percent tax cap levy on all municipalities throughout the state. This was in exchange for the continuation of rent controls in New York City. School districts were limited to how much they could raise the tax levy each year. Prior, there was no such limit on the tax rate. Further a budget vote that was defeated resulted in a 0 percent spending increase. Previously a twice defeated budget could increase spending only 2 percent this issue is hampering budgets as the cap percentage is tied to the wealth of a district as well. In Green Island, a lotto winner is dramatically affecting the school district wealth factor. In many places the budget increase for tax levy does not cover the cost of contract obligations and pension/health care increases (Sipple and Yao, 2015).

Then Governor Cuomo has been quoted as saying "Merge if you can't afford it (Gormley, 2013)." The then governor was implying that if a local community could no longer afford to tax themselves to support their public school, they should consolidate with a neighbor. Howley et al. (2011) indicated that "state level consolidation proposals appear to serve a public relations purpose in times of fiscal crises, rather than substantive fiscal or educational purpose" (p. 12).

Within New York State, the previous governor was pushing a pro-business agenda, and has actively sought to reduce public expenses for state government and local government by asking for a cap on superintendent salaries, a commission that would eliminate expensive union contracts, and negotiating increased public union contributions for health care and a reduction in salary for two years among the two major state unions. The state has also faced significant economic damage in the wake of three major weather events in the past two years. The first two affected the southern tier and the Catskills, and the third was a direct blow to the City of New York and Long Island. The multi-billion-dollar effort to recover has caused the state to seek aid from the federal government. This is compounding the effects the state still suffers from the September 11, 2001, attacks that resulted in a loss of significant tax revenues and damage expenditures to lower Manhattan. Many large companies that are financial traders left the New York metro area for Connecticut and New Jersey. Yet, Yinger (2020) and research associates have found in their research that consolidation does not necessarily reduce cost, for local communities. The research by Yinger (2020) and others has called into question the accepted wisdom of consolidation as a "silver bullet" that will reduce operational expenses and improve achievement in rural schools. So then, how do we examine a major historical event, and how does history reveal the problems which Kingdon, Pressman and Wildavsky, and Ellis describe to us? Did a policy solution in search of a problem emerge? How did local residents thwart state policy implementation? Do my own experiences align with others?

HERKIMER COMMUNITY

The village offers several amenities that would be expected for the capital of an upstate county. This includes a hospital, medium sized commercial district, and a daily newspaper. The village is home to Herkimer County Community College, a two-year liberal arts community college of the State University of New York System. It serves mostly local population with some efforts made to enroll students in distance learning courses through the SUNY Learning Network. The school system itself is supported by state aid (60%) and local taxpayers (35%). The district recruits many of its teachers from the SUNY Oneonta and SUNY Cortland campuses. These are local teacher education schools that are part of the SUNY system. The starting pay for teachers is $37,000, advancing to $57,000. This is slightly lower than the statewide average (information obtained from the school district reorganization study).

When the school district was created in the 1950s under the centralization effort, there was little opposition from the village and surrounding Common Schools. The village offered the area's high school educational program. Herkimer Central School District is composed of two buildings, a K-6 elementary school and a 7–12 high school. Its student population was 1315 students at the time of the proposed reorganization. The district's mascot is The Magician. Organized sporting events have occurred in Herkimer since the 1890s with a fierce rivalry between Herkimer and Ilion on the record since 1893 (Doukas, 2003). Historically, Herkimer Central School emerged from the World War II era Master Plan for School District Reorganization (1947). Ilion Central School was also first proposed in the 1947 Master Plan.

District demographics are changing, with an increased number of students seeking free and reduced lunch, an indicator of increased poverty. This mirrors a nationwide trend, especially in rural areas, where the cheap housing and access to social services of the rural country's capital city makes the area attractive to those in need (Davidson, 1996, pp. 69–87). The district is mostly homogenous with 95 percent of the population reporting itself as white. The Mohawk Valley, in which Herkimer is situated, is considered one of the economically depressed parts of New York State, with an above average unemployment rate reported in the 2010 census figures. Doukas (2003) reviewed the history of the areas and found significant economic decline in the area following systematic manufacturing closures, thereby creating generational poverty as a large manufacturer withdrew, and state economic investment did not replace lost local tax revenue.

RESEARCH PROCESS

Treating the internet-based discussion threads, and the materials uploaded to the internet by newspapers and the school district as archival sources, as Romein et al. (2020) describe as "born digital historical sources" I proceeded to undertake a discourse analysis (Gee, 2014), using Saldania (2021) suggestions for creating a first iteration of coding. I then underwent a second round of coding by creating patterns and relationships between the materials across three sources. While I found that the school officials, and the newspapers were heavily invested in pro consolidation efforts, the community was divided.

What were reasons for the Herkimer community to vote down State policy implementation? Were my experiences, as Ellis et al. (2011) discussed, relevant?

RESULTS FROM ONLINE DISCUSSION

Four areas emerged from the analysis. First, identity emerged as one area of concern about the potential impact of consolidation on the community. Second, economics and money became apparent, especially with questions surrounding salaries and benefits for public employees. Third, programmatic enhancements emerged as a question about what a consolidation would add to the school. Fourth, the specter of state-mandated consolidation emerged, especially as participants were concerned that their voices would be eliminated.

IDENTITY

One reason the rural population of Herkimer may be interested in keeping control of its school district is the notion of the governing structure close to the citizenry. Schools are examples of a governing structure that people wish to have close to where they live (Cornell, 1999). For many parents, the idea of the school system being close and responsive to their needs is an important consideration for where a parent buys their house (Galvin, 2000). A significant number of the posts were critical of the Herkimer community for not voting to merge. One such quote indicated the voters made a bad decision "The cap ain't coming off and 2% won't cut it. People in town are ready to vote everything and anything down" (post 8 BOASF). Another contributor indicated the economic realities of the Mohawk valley are poor, and the district has become too dependent on government aid "The valley has been in decline for the past 40 years . . . we are a society of entitlements . . . the anti-merger group wanted more state aid, sounds like asking for a hand out to me" (post 18 BOASF). The parents of the community were also called out for voting against the merger "The parents who know their kids aren't good enough to compete in real competitive sports voted to keep a mediocre school with lousy academics just so Johnny doesn't sit on the bench" (post # 15 IU76TU). Other people were concerned that local business was afraid of losing customers. Some of the posts felt that people were not thinking through all of the possibilities and were influenced by fear: "mob mentality ruled that vote and sent education in Herkimer back 15 years. I hope they are proud of themselves" (post 31 C4f21).

ECONOMICS AND MONEY

Economics and money seemed to form significant portions of the on-line discussion. First, some of the posts indicated the district's residents would face a loss of value in their housing if the merger went through and the local high school was closed and converted into a 5–6 building. (Ferris, 2012) Second, trust is apparently a significant issue among the on-line participants. Warren (1999) found in multiple instances, trust among the electors and the elected was lacking, especially at the local level. In many posts, the board of education's decision making was called into question. Some of the contributions questioned the reasons the board members were seeking office. "You would find it extremely difficult to find them without a connection to the payroll. Its always been easy. Follow the money" (post 1, MRDNH4). In three instances, outright fraud was alleged by people who posted on the discussion website. "Just wanted to say that when I went to vote in Herkimer I noticed the paper under the vote levers were moved over so that it said yes under the no lever" (post 1 SOCQ6). The discussion fell into three large categories: superintendent salaries, teacher salaries and benefits, and the programmatic loss that the school would face without the merger. The first area of concern posts identified was the superintendent salary. "I'm thinking it should pay NO more than 100k to start" (post 3 NIIHU5). Further down, a contributor raised this point concerning the economics of the district and pay: "'They' say we live in a 'poor' district but in the same breath they will tell you that the pay is in line with other districts" (post 6 NIIHU5). A disconnect exists in the mind of the contributor between the public assertions of poverty and the pay rate of the superintendent. Other posts indicated the pay scale of administrators is too high for a community such as Herkimer. The interim superintendent was making $500 day, which is slightly less than average compared to the rest of upstate New York. It is interesting to note that the posts were interspersed with some contributors who were concerned a district like Herkimer could not attract a sufficiently talented administrator to run the district at the pay level that some people were proposing. Because the superintendent of Herkimer was an interim at the time of the consolidation study, some members of the Herkimer community felt the Ilion superintendent was looking for a way to raise his salary by adding Herkimer to the consolidation study: "Suddenly wonderful Cosimo saw a bigger pay scale for himself and came to

Herkimer too. Stop saying the state came to us or the state is making us!!!" (post #13 712IE).

Some of the posts indicated people did not believe the school was in poor financial shape. For many contributors, the school could not be suffering if the teacher salaries and benefits package remained as lucrative as was made public during the consolidation study. "Have the teachers contribute to healthcare, benis and retirement" (post #4 HEO9I). Other examples further along demanded to know why the children were losing programming, but the pay and benefits packages were staying the same "It's so easy to place blame when you are unwilling to give up anything for yourself, yet you expect the kids' things to be taken away so you can continue with your guilded paychecks and benefits packages" (post 17 HEO9I). In another post, a contributor raised the question of why the teachers were not willing to accept a pay freeze: "how about a pay freeze, or a pay cut? Or a 2% reduction in benefits that rivals most teachers salary or a copy??" (post 8 C42F1).

A second group of contributors were concerned that the school district should attempt to cut expenditures before seeking to merge. The posts were concerned that the teacher's union, specifically, did not pay for any portion of the health care plan that the district provided to its professional staff. Further, post contributors identified teacher salaries as a large expenditure within the district's structure. Several posts felt the teaching staff should take a 10 percent cut in pay in order to ensure that programs were saved, and that students were provided with opportunities within school and extracurricular activities. Other posts indicated the pay of stipends was high and that teachers should volunteer time to ensure that students received sports and arts programs. One post questioned the entire premise of paying teachers for extra duties. The individual felt that teachers were hypocritical by advocating for the merger, yet not willing to sacrifice income in order to ensure students received adequate opportunities for extracurricular offerings. The last major subtheme concerning teachers and their pay involved teaching assignments. Some posts questioned the need to give teachers any break or planning period during the day. There was a question among one of the posts why teachers were given so many perks. The author of the posts stated that Walmart does not provide employees the level of unsupervised activity that teachers receive. This is an interesting comparison, of teaching as a low-level service industry job. Teachers as a group have undertaken strenuous efforts to raise the profession to a high-status occupation. Yet the general population defines teaching as a low-level profession (Cramer, 2016; McHenry-Sorber and Schafft, 2015; Rousmaniere, 2013). This may be due to its status as an entry profession for members of the working-class seeking entry to middle-class status (Labaree, 2008). Teachers are also viewed as lower qualified for professional work, as the media and scholarly reports the low level of standardized test scores of teachers in college. Third, teachers are mostly women, who have historically been viewed as auxiliary to the wage economy. Lois Weis (1990), in her *Working Class Without Work* showed the low esteem teachers received in an urbanized community, where a high school drop-out received higher wages than a teacher with a college degree. Since the economy has restructured to a more knowledge-centered economy, many formally working- and middle-class blue-collar workers have suddenly seen their scant paychecks falling as taxes are used to pay ever wealthier teachers in their communities.

PROGRAM ENHANCEMENT

There was very little discussion about program enhancement for the merger. In many instances, the discussion revolved around what programs would be lost by Herkimer because of the merger failure. People were concerned that the school would lose Kindergarten and some sports, but many could not see what additional programs would be affected by the failed merger vote. One post put it succinctly "Sports, music, Kindergarten-goodbye" (post 10 6c42F1). One person did ask "How do you put together three failing districts, keep all of the staff, give them a 10–12% raise and that equals higher test scores? What were you hoping for fencing? Harry Potter Club? Swim team?50 new lame nonsense electives?" (post #19LR6P0). From this post, it seems evident some members of the community felt the newly consolidated district was moving beyond the provision of academic services that were comfortable and justifiable to members of the community. This echoes research by Berkman (2005) and Peshkin (1978) conducted that indicated the schools were willing to provide some but not everything to students.

STATE MANDATED

As in other areas of the country, residents in Herkimer feared the state would somehow mandate consolidation. The posts that were reviewed contained some level of understanding that the state, as part of the education policy setter, was looking to change the role of local school districts in New York. One post indicated "Too late, the boat has sailed, Herkimer will be annexed [by a neighboring district] one the state steps in" (post 28 C42f1). Other people raised concerns that the state could not be trusted, and that the promises of extra aid once the consolidation was passed were faulty . . . "where do you think the state was going to [get] the money to give for the merge? TAXES" (post 28 IU76TU). Other posts indicated the state would no longer trust local taxpayers in running their own school districts: "Maybe the state will just step in and merge them all anyway. Take it out of the taxpayer's hands. Do what is best for all school districts" (post 17 SOCQ6). Another person wondered about the state government priority in its budget. "If Albany can find 30% to add to the state pension fund it doesn't seem so difficult to fund our children's education does it? Because after all . . . Its about the kids right?" (post #11 712 IE). Another person put the blame for the current fiscal environment clearly on the state: "it is due to less and less aid and more and more unfunded mandates put on the schools" (post #21 HEO9I). It is evident from the sample of responses that some community members believe the school system is in danger due to state budgetary and policy decisions and not local actions. A divisiveness between rural communities and state government concerning school governance is historical, and continuously simmering (Jakubowski, 2020a; Jakubowski, 2021). The division could partially be due to the lack of trust that many people in rural areas have for government outside of the local area. Justice (2014) found the role of the Commissioner of Education's representative to local school districts was viewed as a spy, and in many ways, the local citizens only wanted the state level government involved if there was a conflict that could not be settled locally.

With the increasing role the state is playing in testing districts, and identifying them as in need of improvement, many local members of the community feel that the state is already interfering with their local efforts in education. In many ways, Theobald (1997) captured the stresses between the local government and its desire to control the schools in a local fashion and the state government. At the state level, the government is concerned about the schools as an economic and competitive resource for the future. State-mandated consolidation is viewed as one way to end problems in local school communities that have hurt students and the community at large (Sunderman et al., 2017). The residents locally were concerned that if they did not solve their educational and financial problems internally, the state would take action, and merge the district as a solution.

In New York, the office of Commissioner of Education has not shied away from removing the entire board of education of a school district (Roosevelt), reinstating Superintendent (Hempstead) or issuing a state mandated improvement plan that the board of education, under orders from the commissioner must follow (Wyandanch). The state law 310 appeals process also grants the commissioner the power to overturn local board decisions. It is not beyond reason to believe that a commissioner could remove schools that are no longer large enough to educate their populations.

A special note, with the COVID-19 pandemic raging, and state-imposed mandates on schools, including remote learning, vaccinations and masks, outright opposition has emerged, with local boards of education meetings becoming battlegrounds between people in opposition to the mandates, and board officials and administrators who are tasked with implementation and enforcement (Kamenetz, 2021). The battles are part of a larger national political battle between members of communities who believe in and support the role of the Biden administration and state government mandates to slow the spread of COVID-19, and as Longhurst (2020) pointed out, those who believe the election was a sham, and in response do not believe that the government is valid in its policy decisions.

CAUTIONARY CONSIDERATIONS

While this study is an attempt at unique content analysis of an untapped resource in the on-going school consolidation debate, there are three major limits to the study: self-selection nature, inability to follow up for clarification, inability to control for multiple identities for one informant. The voluntary nature of online comment boards, and the technology needed in order to participate, establishes a scenario where only the people who have computers and an internet modem are sampled in this study. Further, people within the jurisdiction may have an opinion about the merger but are not sampled within this survey unless they went online to comment. Additionally, there is no way to see if the participants in the online discussion board are representative of the population demographically.

A second limitation of the study is the inability to follow-up on statements that are posted online. In other forms of information gathering, the investigator can contact participants for follow up immediately through the interview process, or later as part of a data review. An informant may not have utilized precise language in describing an idea that is interpreted by the researcher after the fact to mean an idea completely different than the intended one. This limitation is faced by historians reviewing documents that are decades, if not centuries old. Usually, historians will make professional judgments and seek additional information to support the hypothesis or refute it as necessary (Lowenthal, 1998).

A third limitation of the study is the inability to control for multiple identities attributed to one person. Because the site does not have a unique IP user identification system, it is possible a person could register as multiple different users to comment on the topic of conversation without a researcher knowing this was the case. That individual would then have given themselves more weight to the discussion than other participants. As social media grows in use, some of the people are earlier adaptors and utilize the technology with frequency and enthusiasm. The role of internet usage is generational as well. Recent popular studies have indicated adolescents are moving away from email and Facebook to newer forms of online communication. Some important information may not have been sampled because alternative sources of online information were not sampled. This includes Facebook, Myspace, Instagram, Twitter, Snapchat and blog posts that are created by users and exist independently of the TOPIX website.

While the study does contain three limitations, the information that was gathered has use for administrators and researchers seeking explanations for this very important topic. Further research should explore the use of online data that is enhanced by other instruments to gather data. Other reviews of this information may benefit from utilizing programs designed to analyze words and phrases that are included within the online informal discussion and materials presented in the traditional media or formal venues.

CHAPTER CONCLUSIONS

Four areas of consolidation literature have dominated the narrative in examining and evaluating the policy implementation process of educational improvement which is often defeated at the local level: identity, cost efficiency, program enhancement, and state mandates. I think it is time that researchers need to shift the research beyond these areas. First, data selections in past studies usually privileged narratives which emerged from the local elite, those who were in a space of power or influence. Yet using online methods, we can overcome what Duncan (1999) and Sherman (2021) found, the reluctance of people who were not in power to talk to outsiders. Realistically, people are often concerned with the impact of their communication with outsiders, especially if they are socially or economically, or educationally vulnerable (Carr and Kefalas, 2009).

Some of the findings within this study support the previously published literature concerning the role of identity, but it was not as central as expected when stakeholder opposition using nontraditional means was measured. The findings from the study indicate it was a combination of areas that resulted in the people of Herkimer voting the merger down: a lack of trust in the elected officials on the Board of Education; a cognitive disconnect between the public assertions of poverty and the salaries and benefits package the district offered to administration and teachers, a belief that more could be done before a merger was a viable option, and finally, a lack of trust in the state following up on its promises to provide additional funding after the merger.

An area of concern to the local population was the state mandating mergers. One of the most poignant posts came from an astute observer who suggested: the state of New York suggested hospitals merger, then mandated they will. Schools are not far behind. This concern about the level of government involvement in public schools is a manifestation of how important schools are to local communities' economic, social, political, and future wellbeing.

Research in the future should look at additional case studies of online consolidations and see if the patterns are similar in the print literature. One theory that should be explored is the role the traditional media plays in establishing discussion agendas (Langer and Gruber, 2021). In many local reorganizations, the print media tends to focus on identity and sports. A second theory should be tested involving the differences between anonymous websites and identifiable websites. If people can be attributed to statements, does this alter their levels of participation or the commentary on the topics that they comment on?

Finally, many school administrative training courses will need to discuss how social media and unregulated websites affect policy directives within education. As the internet becomes the de facto news production agency for school districts, leaders will need to become more astute in monitoring the posts and ensuring the district can react to rumors and incorrect information as it is posted on the web. Blogging and Twitter have become one of the most important news sources in present day America. Facebook and social media are credited with changing the political landscape of the Middle East. Schools need to be as aware of the power of the web in their operations.

Chapter 3

Lakeside Conflict

Schools have been portrayed as the heart of rural communities in literature, art, and popular culture (Fitchen, 1991; Hasnat et al., 2021; Lyson, 2002; Miller, 2021; Theobald, 1997). Schooling children is one of the fundamental responsibilities of a community as defined by the early Massachusetts government (Kaestle, 1983; Katz, 1987; Tyack and Cuban, 1997; Taylor, 2002). When changing circumstances place school community dynamics in an upheaval, the discussion is public and full of emotions (Jakubowski, 2019; Jakubowski, 2021; Justice, 2004; McHenry-Sorber and Schafft, 2015; Spring, 1997). The purpose of this chapter is to examine one such change in dynamics in the western New York region. A small rural school district partnered with another smaller rural school district to examine consolidation. The consolidation effort failed, and the online discussion listed several reasons for the failure. I compared the locally cited reasons for the failure to scholarly literature that identified reasons for school merger failure across the nation (Bard et al., 2006; Castle, 1995; DeYong and Howley, 1990; Peshkin, 1978; Peshkin, 1982; Schmuck and Schmuck, 1992; Steele, 2010; Tangorra, 2013; Theobald, 1995; Williams, 2013). Using Ellis's et al. (2011) autoethnography, I wanted to compare what happened to these two communities to my own experience in a defeated merger attempt. As I discussed in chapter 2, I examined Kingdon's (2011) agenda setting research, and created a case study (Stake, 1995) using Gee's (2014) discourse analysis. I posit in this chapter that the potential loss of the high school would profoundly impact the community which voted no. As Lyson (2002) and Sherman and Schafft (2022) point out, the school is much more than just a building in a community. It is an economic engine, a social enterprise, and an identifiable common element. Parshall (2023) described how crucial governments are for local rural areas, and even with proposed lower taxes, and transferred fiscal incentives from the state, many areas choose to keep their government in order to ensure hope that the past economic difficulties are behind them.

COMMUNITY DESCRIPTION

The Western New York Southern Tier area by Lake Erie contains a large area of agriculture in New York's apple and grape regions. Many of the students are mobile in the area, and the unemployment rate is high for their parents. The school communities in this region have experienced significant declines in population, as the commuter centers of Jamestown, Dunkirk, and Buffalo have lost industry. The largest employers in the region, defined as Greater Chautauqua County include the state, SUNY College at Fredonia, and the Dunkirk and Jamestown regional medical centers. It is an economically depressed region that has been in recession or slow growth for well over thirty years (Craig, 2016; Rasmussen, 2009). The Appalachian Regional Commission (ARC) of which Chautauqua County is part of, has identified the region's per capita income, unemployment status, and other economic measures as underperforming for the state (ARC data, 2022).

The two schools subject to this study, Brocton Central School District and Westfield Academy and Central School District, have long histories of providing education to their communities. According to the 1947 Master Plan for School District Reorganization, Brocton centralized in August of 1938, reflecting a Great Depression era centralization to ease economic burden on local populations. Westfield, was proposed as a district centering on the Academy, formed in 1837 (Beigh, 2018). Westfield history resources indicate an elementary level log cabin was established in 1802 for the area's children. In 1946, Westfield centralized, and the 1958 plan called for the addition of Ripley Central School. The 1958 Master Plan recommended Brocton and Fredonia consolidate. Each school district experienced an increase in population following World War II and expanded their school's physical plants to accommodate the student needs. The Westfield and Brockton communities established strong sports programs and became the center of musical performance and community events as the schools' provided locations for community groups to host activities at the facilities.

In the late 1970s and early 1980s, the entire region saw a significant decline in population, and the schools became increasingly dependent on state aid for operational expenses. The two communities changed demographically, as Westfield maintained middle class status, while Brockton became increasingly working class, with some diversity from Dunkirk and the surrounding farming communities. Both districts began to explore consolidation studies with surrounding communities. In each instance these attempts were defeated at the polls. In 2012, Brockton explored a consolidation with Fredonia. Westfield explored consolidation with Ripley. Both mergers were defeated. Later that year, the board of education of Brockton approached Westfield in the hopes of consolidating into one school district. Simultaneously, a bill was introduced into the New York State legislature that would allow schools to establish a regional high school without following through with the merger process. Local schools would keep their elementary and middle schools, and would be, under the proposal, able to combine into regional schools that would offer a general, non-specialized curriculum. With this background, the debate in the Brockton-Westfield community over a school consolidation provides an interesting snapshot into a local community decision-making process.

Five major categories emerged from the online threads which captured what people were communicating across the internet about the school reorganization plan. These five topics include:

1. a post related to a school building or the physical structure
2. a post concerning money
3. an attack—*ad hominem* or otherwise related to attacking a group
4. a post related to the state, state policies, or the state government
5. a post relating to the region or regionalization.

THE COMMUNITY'S DISCUSSION

Online discussion revealed that people indicated three major flaws with the consolidation study that would result in the failure of the process. First, the contributors often said that they believed that the tax rates were too high, and that the consolidation would not save enough money. Under the subset of money, posts often included statements that contributors felt the school buildings would pose a barrier to consolidation. One post stated "people in the village want their kids to walk to school." This statement is interpreted as indicating any need to bus students to the partner community would result in opposition. Other contributors indicated the previous mergers in the area and across the state had resulted in additional expenses to district taxpayers in the newly formed district. This fear of expenses is an important concern among taxpayers in the region. New York State has been cited as one of the highest taxed regions in the US. The State governor has attempted to address this concern by limiting tax increases in school districts to less than 2 percent to limit increased spending. The fear expressed online also runs counter to one of the central points of the consolidation study that pointed to taxpayer savings in a successful consolidation.

Second, several contributors felt other alternatives were still available and should be explored. One post stated "make a regional high school at Chautauqua." This post was directly referencing the work that the local legislative representative was undertaking to gain approval for a regional high school. Another post recommended that the community should consolidate with the four surrounding schools that were in northern Chautauqua County. Another person indicated that the community had lost its opportunity to consolidate when the Brocton-Fredonia consolidation was defeated and that the school district (Brockton) should be broken up divided between the two contiguous districts. This was not a popular proposal. One recommendation that received some positive support would have tuition high school students from Brockton to one of the surrounding districts of the parent's choice. The contributions to the online discussion raise the issue of how the community engagement committee explored options during the process. This concern is raised throughout the conversation about how thoroughly the members of the committee studied the school. This discussion echoes the statewide debate that radical reform in school organization is necessary, as members of the educational leadership have been quoted as saying "the current structure of schooling makes no sense."

The third major reason that the posters gave for why the consolidation process would fail is trust. Throughout the thread, issues of trust in all different levels of the process emerged. One comment was particularly pointed against the administrative staff, asserting that "the leaders are greedy." Another comment asserted that the board of education members did not have the community interest in the forefront of the discussion. Other comments questioned if all the information was truly being shared with the community. Further comments indicated the online participants questioned the state. The comments posted expressed a belief that the state would "renig (sic) on merger money . . . they are bankrupt." Another post indicated the state was "just going to force us to merge anyway." This lack of trust between community leaders and members of the community echoes a larger trend in the decreased confidence in public officials across the nation. The expenditure of public dollars and the frequent use of executive sessions at school meetings frustrates community members who feel transparency in government is important. New York State, in general, does not rank highly on national surveys of government transparency, and the local concern over transparency may be citizens reflecting this statewide issue locally.

During the time of this consolidation attempt, local state representatives were championing legislation which would have reauthorized the exploration of regional schools, like some legacy districts in Long Island. The bill unfortunately was blocked (Dunkirk Observer, 2013). Other members of the online community believed the solution of a consolidation would cause another problem, namely increased costs to taxpayers. With such opposition to the proposed policy solution, the political stream should be examined.

The political stream happens simultaneously with the problem and policy stream. Politics is defined as the allocation of resources by the act of negotiation through power (Kingdon, 2011, p. 145). In the context of the consolidation study in the Brocton-Westfield area, the political stream demonstrated a significant clash between two groups of stakeholders. The first group believed that the combined community would benefit from the consolidation. The proposal in the consolidation study for board of education seats, school location, and combining resources between the two communities argued that the plan would not adversely affect Brockton or Westfield. This group of stakeholders was actively promoting the findings within the study of reduced tax rates, enhanced educational programs, improved facilities, and the ability to recruit young families to the district.

The second group believed the consolidation process would result in a political loss for their community that was unacceptable. This group was composed of several subgroups that cited different reasons for not supporting the consolidation. One such group in Brockton was called "Save our Schools" and used the internet, public protests, and letter writing campaigns to sway the population in their community. This group cited the loss of a building within one community, which they claimed would deprive the community of their identity. Another reason the group cited was the feeling that Westfield looked down on Brockton, and their children would not have access to all educational opportunities in the new school. The group insisted the loss of the school in Brockton would hurt the business community in the area. The SOS group wanted the Brockton schools to investigate other policy options, such as cutting spending, increasing the tax rate, or seeking other ways to attract additional support from the state.

Another subgroup opposed to the consolidation policy solution was the group calling for regionalization. While not organized like SOS, this subgroup coalesced around the idea that efficiency and opportunity would come from a regional high school or working with additional schools in the area. While no one person was a leader or organized rallies and political action, the subgroup influenced the discussion of consolidation as the only feasible option. This influence caused citizens to question the consolidation study committee and ask if the group had entertained all possible solutions. Their activity raised doubt among the online community, and within the traditional print media that consolidation was the correct solution for the schools.

The citizens in Westfield and Brocton failed to reach consensus on the policy solution and political stream in solving their problem of a school losing funding and unable to provide effective educational programs. Because the voters within the two communities could not see the consolidation as the best, most acceptable policy solution, the consolidation process failed. The window for consolidation had again passed the Westfield and Brocton communities. The failure of consolidation in two communities that have identified repeatedly a need to change their organizational structure raises further questions about the process as prescribed by state law as a solution to declining enrollments and funding.

These events, when compared to my own experiences (Ellis et al., 2011) are relevant. In the centralization event I witnessed, the people in Little Valley were concerned that the Cattaraugus residents would "look down" on their children. The residents who supported the centralization of Little Valley were tired of the endless cycle of merger studies, which often happened almost cyclically, with fluctuations in state aid a major cause. As the Little Valley community continued to explore centralizations with neighboring Randolph, Cattaraugus, Ellicottville, and Salamanca, attitudes towards how other communities viewed the students, and parents, and residents of Little Valley floated into the open. Yet Little Valley is unique, as the Cattaraugus County seat. Therefore, its daytime population was large, as commuters who lived across the region reported for county jobs in the village. Brocton experienced the same events, but was hampered by Lake Erie to its west. Brocton could only partner with Westfield, Fredonia, Cassadaga Valley, and Chautauqua Lake, which had just consolidated less than a decade earlier. Residents in Brocton wanted centralization, but the voters in both Fredonia and Westfield did not, as each proposal created a negative impact on their own community.

After the failure of the Westfield-Brocton centralization, two major issues emerged in the area. First, the Westfield residents were uninterested, based upon a survey, in pursuing a revote with Brocton. The survey cited the economic and community cohesion of Westfield. A second reason for the status quo was the location of the high school. Residents in Westfield concluded that the loss of the physical building (the high school program would move to Brocton) would profoundly hinder families who often combined visits to schools with other shopping and social activities.

The second instance is the continued promotion of centralization/consolidation by the local newspapers/media outlets. The *Dunkirk Observer* and the *Westfield Republican* have both carried frequent editorials which chastise the local residents for failing to support reorganizations. The paper has also chastised the New York Legislature for its failure to authorize the regional high school process. The editorials support the efforts of Ripley to tuition students to the Chautauqua Lake School District. A supportive theme in the paper created a positive report on the combination of "back room" supported by local schools and BOCES.

CONCLUSION

With the local newspapers' pro consolidation in Chautauqua County, but residents unwilling in some of the communities to vote yes, the school districts have become creative in how they will "survive" as one superintendent reported in an interview. Ripley has begun paying tuition for their high school students to attend the nearby Chautauqua Lake School District. The local Board of Cooperative Educational Services, or BOCES, is offering additional programs, and cooperative purchasing for districts to share costs. The area has explored the creation of virtual high schools, providing educational programming online, as the COVID-19 pandemic showed as one potential alternative. Community members are adamant that the crisis point, or focusing event has not emerged, and that internal options are still readily available. Until the focusing event, or crisis becomes bluntly apparent, residents will continue to vote no, not to save their identity or mascot, but because fundamental questions are yet to be answered.

Chapter 4

Leadership's Dissonance on School Reform

Policy decisions by New York State for the past 100 years have identified, and especially since 1958, codified into law and policy reorganization as the acceptable solution to improve rural school, as metrocentric and urban normative bureaucrats describe rural areas in deficit terms. Two areas, reducing the administrative costs associated with operating a smaller district (efficiency), and enhancing the educational program (effectiveness) are the two central points of rhetoric out of Albany. Yet this is in direct opposition to federal and state policy that has increasingly called for the dissolution of large comprehensive urban schools. Federal Race to the Top and Every Student Succeeds Act legislation as implemented by the New York State Education policy calls for reforming urban schools by creating smaller schools that are no larger than many of the rural districts that are called to merge in order to create efficiencies. This urban normative approach (Fulkerson and Thomas, 2019) only serves to reinforce to rural residents a perception that their needs are secondary (Trujilllo, 2021).

Does the urbanormativity stem from the bureaucracy, the leadership, or the lack of understanding rural areas? The purpose of this chapter is to explore the role of current state policy in encouraging rural school consolidations while pushing for large urban schools to dissolve into a multitude of smaller schools. The reactions of rural schools to the increased difficulties presented by declining resources will be explored. Further implications for research and policy will be discussed.

THE ROAD TO THE PRESENT

This is not the first time rural schools have been called upon to consolidate in the Empire State. Rather, it is a continuation in a long-standing policy in

New York State to merge smaller schools and create what reformers have called "the one best system" of schools modeled on urban reform movements of previous decades (Tyack and Cuban, 1997).

As the newly formed State Education Department after 1898, the popular and most accepted thinking at the time was that consolidations in rural areas would solve the perceived problems (Loveland, 1993). The first three Commissioners of Education, utilizing their role as a local and national authority about school reforms, emphasized rural one room schoolhouses must consolidate into larger organizational units (Gettleman, 1969; Loveland, 1993). In some ways, the department was successful, as one and two room Common Schools, or educational districts in rural New York who did not provide a junior or senior high education, centralized into comprehensive districts which provided elementary and secondary education (Parkerson and Parkerson, 2015). Taking their lead from reformers, such as Cubberly (1914), the New York State Leadership identified, in their opinion, significant issues with rural schools. This included poor instruction, poor hygiene, poor fiscal support, and a desire to thwart the reform attempts by Albany-based leadership (Chiles, 2018; Heffernan, 2021; Justice, 2012). Yet rural residents objected to these pronouncements, and instead asked the state leadership to understand local conditions, and local realities. With the Great Depression from 1928–1941, rural farmers and business leaders were often faced with the inability to raise sufficient funds to support schools. As Steffes (2008) identified, the State of New York began to offer aid to localities as a way of improving education programming. One of the side effects of the additional state-based aid to local schools was the demand to change practice in local areas. The aid often resulted in changes to the length of the school term, as more educational time in schools became a constant demand, with a minimum of 180 days the 2021 mandate. The second side effect of additional aid were changes to curriculum. The State used aid to unify standardized curriculum in areas in the areas covered by the Regents exams.

As Folts (1996) described in the History of the University of the State of New York and State Education Department, the 1920s and 1930s were especially difficult, as rural areas were under profound economic distress. Folts indicated that the State began to increasingly fund rural education, and proceeded to try and find a way to increase efficiency and effectiveness in the programming. As Chiles (2018) described, Governor Alfred Smith used the increase in state aid to local districts as a hallmark of his governorship, and later presidential aspirations. The aid top districts began to increase the credentialing of local teachers, as minimum requirements were increased (Parkerson and Parkerson, 2015).

During World War II, as the nation fought against fascism in Europe and Asia, the New York State legislature launched a commission to accomplish a comprehensive review and reform of schools in New York State. The Rapp Couldet commission explored centralized goals of improving educational offerings, improving teacher training, redirecting taxes towards more efficient usage, and creating what they considered as modern buildings (Folts, 1996; Gamson and Hodge, 2016; Jakubowski, 2021). As the war ended, the commission published its first Master Plan for School District Reorganization (1947) and the State Education Department, under the leadership of Commissioner Francis Spaulding (1967) continued to push for district consolidation. The Rapp-Cauldet Commission's reports established some basic principles of what was, in the State's opinion, an efficient school district.

The interim reports of the Commission provide a set of principles, and the "best" thinking of the time period. These interim reports were later combined into the Master Plan of 1947. First, the program must include a school providing grade 1–12 education. Kindergartens were introduced post World War II. Second, the district must not be physically too large, and transportation time from home to school was suggested at no more than an hour. Third, the district must have a balance between village and rural farming, and should have shared viewpoints and characteristics across the community. Fourth, a minimum of 1000 students should be enrolled in the district, grades 1–12. Finally, the taxes collected should ensure an adequate program for learners in traditional, commercial, and work-related training.

After the development of suburbia, in the post–World War II population boom, and school construction explosion, the State was again faced with a need to create a comprehensive plan for reorganizing the still unconsolidated Common Schools. As Spaulding (1967) had expressed in his writings and speeches until his death, parents wanted progress, and the nation needed science and technology in the classroom. To that end, a second commission published a revised Master Plan for School District Reorganization in 1958, considering advances in auto transportation, suburban growth, and the creation of newer, more safe highways which made travel between communities safer and quicker (Jakubowski, 2020a).

The Plan's goals continued to call for enhanced programmatic offerings and create a better, improved, and fiscally stable system (Haller and Monk, 1988). In many places of the state, the changes which emerged in the residential patterns in post–World War II era saw continued growth in the inner ring suburbs, the creation of BOCES to service suburban and rural schools, and increased population movement away from farms to the urban areas of the state. Essert and Howard (1952) created a study that examined the best practices in the state for combining small, rural communities into Centralized School Districts that would promote educational effectiveness and efficiencies. Their efforts were a chronicling and a list of suggestions for superintendents looking for ways to improve the chances of merging the common schools into centralized school districts. Essert and Howard (1952) specifically called on district leaders to take their message to the people in their homes, at their farms, and at their places of work. The 1958 Master Plan also called for community leaders to support the work of the Commission locally. The finalized report indicates that members of the Commission came from across the state, and the latest scientific and educational theories, along with transportation and financial experts contributed to the Commission.

As the economy in New York ebbed and flowed, from the 1960s through the 1980s, rural school consolidation attempts continued across New York State (Canter, 1986; Haller and Monk, 1988; Monk and Haller, 1986; Sher and Tompkins, 1986; Woodward, 1986). One reason consolidation attempts may have slowed down was a change in state law which permitted school districts to undertake building projects without directly tying the efforts to implementing the Master Plan. Previously, districts identified in the Master Plan for reorganization were mandated to justify to the State Education Department, why the building project was critical (Szuberla et al., 2002). Before this legislative change, the only feasible path for many rural communities to expand, rebuild, or alter their school physical plan was a successful consolidation.

One group active in showing rural and small schools could do more with less was the Catskill Rural Project, based out of SUNY Oneonta. The study council provided research reports on all manner of rural issues, including leadership, teaching, teacher aides in the classroom, building design, and other advice and best practices. The study council, still presently active, was recognized nationally as a resource, and leader in identifying problems, suggesting practices, and communicating solutions to other rural schools (Bohrson, 1962).

Tyack (1972), one of the leaders in research school organizations, described the intensity and divisiveness school consolidation attempts had on rural communities. In a review of consolidation history, Tyack found that resistance to consolidation was strong:

> But patrons continued to resist consolidation and standardization in a battle which made little sense to educators who had preconceived ideas about schooling. Country people may have been dissatisfied with their school buildings and with an archaic curriculum, but they wanted to control their own schools. In a major study of rural schools in New York State in 1921, for example, 65 per cent of rural patrons polled wanted to elect their county superintendent; 69 per cent opposed consolidation of schools. (Tyack, 1972, p. 17)

Rural residents wanted the right to exercise controlling their own schools. Community agency in face of state demands for "reform." Yet the push for consolidation as reform continued despite almost 30 percent of residents opposing successful consolidations (Anrig, 1963, p. 162). The State leadership continued to promote the policy, despite opposition from communities.

In the 1990s, the governor of New York called for the Commissioner of Education to update the Master plan to "consolidate inefficient jurisdictions. The study was to provide for a list of school districts to be targeted for consolidation" (Wiles, 1994 p. 299). While the plan was published by the Board of Regents, the political implications damaged both the schools and the Commissioner of Education during that time period. Calling forth regional leadership of the BOCES District Superintendents, the committees examined the economic and programmatic offerings of the smallest (usually under 3500 student districts). When the report was presented to the Board of Regents, the political uproar was significant. The small school districts have always been threatened by the specter of consolidation looming over their existence.

LEADERSHIP CALLS FOR CONSOLIDATION IN 2000s

As the budget debates in New York have become increasingly difficult since the stock market crash of 2008 (Sipple and Yao, 2015), the leadership have called forth three major commissions to address the rise in property taxes faced by the citizens in New York. In 2008, then Governor Elliot Spitzer empaneled a commission chaired by Thomas Suozzi, a Long Island County Executive to examine the role of property taxes in the state of New York. The Commission, after a series of statewide hearings and reports, issued a recommendation for the implementation of a property tax cap, that would in essence prevent a local municipality, such as a school district, from raising tax rates above a percentage of last year's tax rates (Suozzi, 2008). In 2008, the Lundine Commission also announced, after a series of meetings and reports, a call for consolidation of services by local municipalities. Four recommendations emerged from the commission that would address rising school expenses in New York State: 1) Empower the Commissioner of Education to order consolidations; 2) Set up local schools restructuring committees; 3) Authorize regional collective bargaining contracts; 4) Facilitate the consolidation of back-office services (Suozzi, 2008). After being elected to office, Governor Cuomo has pushed for increased government efficiency, going so far as to implement, with Legislative approval in 2011 (Office of State Comptroller, 2011) a "tax cap" of 2 percent on municipal budgets that require a supermajority of voters to override. In many rural school communities, the implementation of the 2 percent tax cap, and the implementation of a Gap Elimination Adjustment, or GEA reduction in state aid has caused boards of education and superintendents to cut programs and lay off teaching staff.

In some school districts across the state an increased amount of discussion involves the possibility of schools facing bankruptcy (*NY Post*, 2012).

The New York State (NYS) School Boards Association, the NYS Council of School Superintendents, School Administrators Association of New York, and others have called on increase state aid for schools, but the leadership has indicated the proverbial well has run dry. Governor Cuomo stated in March of 2013 "If you are a school district, or a city, or a town or a county, and you are looking for a fundamental financial reform, consolidation is one of the obvious ones" (Gormley, 2013). This is keeping in line with other governor's positions on school spending in different states (McHenry-Sorber, 2009; Shober, 2012) As state expenditures for education rise, many governors are taking increased control in directing their state's education policy. The performance levels of schools within states directly affect other areas of a governor's political agenda. If schools are not successful, the state may have a difficult time attracting and retaining businesses in an era of increased competition.

Second, in the locally based labor market, if the schools do not educate children, the consequences result in workers who are not ready to assume positions of employment in high tech industry sectors. This is an area of concern within New York State, as the Capital region is moving from manufacturing to more nanotechnology creation. Additionally, the former Commissioner of Education, John B. King, Jr. PhD, has stated "If you were drawing it up today, you wouldn't have 700 school districts," (Reilly, 2013). At the November 2012 Board of Regents meeting, Deputy Commissioner Slentz, a former rural school superintendent, recommended the Board of Regents support the following policy proposals for increased efficiency and effectiveness:

- Reorganization through merging of contiguous school districts.
- Regional secondary schools; and
- BOCES as regional leader. (New York State Board of Regents, 2012)

In New York, the Board of Regents sets educational policy for the state and has final jurisdiction over the entire educational system from prekindergarten to adult learning. Their funding and policy recommendations are influential on the state legislators who allocate educational spending in the state of New York. For most of the 2010s, the top political and educational leadership in New York State has called upon small, mostly rural schools to consolidate in order to increase efficiency and effectiveness. Simultaneously, political leadership has tried, unsuccessfully, to reverse the falling demographics and "brain drain" in the rural areas of the state. Over the past three decades, the population of upstate New York has decreased as many manufacturing companies have moved operations overseas or to the south. Large areas of

New York's rural areas have seen rapid decreases in their school-aged populations, and large out migrations in adults who would be childbearing aged (Deitz, 2005; Killeen and Sipple, 2006). As the 2022 Appalachian Rural Commission reported for New York's Southern Tier Counties, the continued economic struggles, population loss, and out flight of residents created significant issues in the area. While the COVID-19 pandemic reversed some of the trends, and housing values in areas which are attractive to remote workers increased, there are still significant issues in counties with high needs (Sherman, 2021). New York has decided in policy to continuously underfund its state University of New York system. For colleges, mostly community colleges and four-year comprehensive programs in the Southern Tier, they are struggling to fulfill their missions, while also recruiting sufficient students and tuition revenue. Chautauqua County hosts two SUNY schools, SUNY Fredonia and Jamestown Community College. In Cattaraugus County, St. Bonaventure is a comprehensive university offering bachelor's and master's degrees. In Alleghany, two private schools, Alfred University and Houghton, are joined by SUNY Alfred State College. Steuben County includes Corning Community College (SUNY), while Chemung County has Elmira College. Tioga County does not have its own higher education institution, sharing the distinction with Chenango County (a branch campus of SUNY Morrisville). Broome County is home to SUNY Binghamton and SUNY Broome Community College. Otsego County includes SUNY Oneonta and Hartwick college. Schoharie County is home to SUNY Cobleskill, while Delaware county has SUNY Delhi. Tompkins County contains Cornell University and Ithaca College, while Cortland County contains Tompkins-Cortland Community College and SUNY Cortland. Schulyer County, one of the smallest in the State, does not have a higher education campus. Proximity to universities and colleges is cited as a pull factor in migration for rural areas, as families and businesses enjoy the social, economic, and status which the schools provide.

Research studies by Carr and Kefalas (2009); Corbett (2007); Miller (2021); and Tieken (2014) have both pointed to the needs in many rural communities for a strong school system, while Theobald (1997) and Zuckerman (2019) have both written about the roles local rural schools could play in revitalizing their communities. Lyson (2002); Miller (2021); Thomas (2003); and Sipple et al. (2019) and have discovered that in communities that have experienced a school consolidation, and lose their school, the community loses some of the attractiveness and services which were formerly provided within the village. In several rural villages, the school forms the center of community life, as it is the entertainment zone for sports and theater, as well as a gathering place for people who are looking to unite behind a common cause. The school and people's identities in many rural areas are intertwined. One factor cited in the failures of school consolidation studies is the loss of identity that prevents voters from approving such measures (Jakubowski, 2019).

As Palmer (2017) found, in examining superintendents' views on meeting the educational needs for their districts following the implemented tax cap, many leaders were concerned that their role devolved into ensuring necessary and mandatory programs were saved. Few leaders expressed optimism considering the constraints on the budget to account for rising costs, from personal to mandatory curriculum changes.

A study on school choice in rural education found that residents who live farthest away from their assigned districts will partake at a higher rate than close by residents. The study found that most students do not, especially in rural areas, partake in school choice, which is one of the mainstays of urban school reform policy in New York. The study indicated that communities in rural areas are often attached to, and engaged with their local school (Edwards, 2021).

With many state reformers viewed as "outsiders" community members are concerned about surrendering their local control over governance structure to another community that may have been at one time a close rival in sports and community boosterish (Cramer, 2016; Reynolds, 1999; Truilijo, 2022). The comparison of rural and urban education policy is not new, and in one study from the early 1970s, rural educators were praised for setting the example for their urban counterparts (Berger, 1972). Yet the examination of rural education for exemplary practices did not convince policy makers to end their consolidation push, even while promoting decentralization in urban areas.

URBAN SCHOOL POLICY—NEW YORK CENTERED

Urban schools, since the mid-1950s, and the "White flight" era, have been identified as failing student's educational needs. Kozol (2005) has published extensively on the plight of urban students in the United States. Political leadership of the United States, as well as New York have called for education reform. Starting in 1989, the State Education Department has identified Schools Under Registration Review (SURR) that are the lowest performing schools in New York State based upon student achievement. SURR schools, mostly concentrated in the large Urban areas, were required to undergo a state review of their educational program, and with local district support, implement significant changes or face revocation of registration by the Board of Regents. After the early Commissioners of Education focused on rural school reform, the change in focus occurred in the 1960s and 1970s, as Nyquist (1969–1976) focused on desegregating New York City. As Murphy (2022) pointed out, Rochester City schools were under significant and profound stress from segregation in the city and the inability of the Rochester Community to work with the surrounding white, middle class suburbs. In 1976, Judge Curtain ordered the Buffalo City Schools to desegregate, but like all of the post-Milikin case northern states, a school district was established as a legal entity and forced cross border transportation was not permitted (Johnson, 2014). I know, and have experience as a suburban student. My mother tells how she, in the 1950s and 1960s attended Catholic school in the South Buffalo area. Reardon and Yun (2002) pointed out how the establishment of religiously operated schools created segregated schools. In the charter school movement, the research is mixed. In response to the profoundly troubling achievement gaps which emerged as a result of defunding urban areas and schools, reform efforts, specifically the School Under Registration Review system of New York State, sent teams of state experts into mostly underperforming urban schools to visit, utilize data. Write a report, and have the district create an improvement plan to ensure the schools and its children would perform better on state assessments (Viteritti, 2001).

In 2001, then President Bush launched the No Child Left Behind Act which authorized a school accountability system based on tests developed at the state level for schools receiving federal Title I funds to assist educating children from high poverty backgrounds. If schools did not meet state established proficiency rates, the Education Department would announce a "School in need of Improvement list." This list, publicized in local media reports, would trigger the implementation of federally required penalties, which included the opportunity for tutoring by an outside vendor or allowing parents to send their child to another public school in the district. If the school did not improve after two years, it was subjected to a Corrective Action that US DOE defined as: "replacing certain staff or fully implementing a new curriculum, while continuing to offer public school choice and supplemental educational services for low-income students" (Ravitch, 2016). The district was required to submit to the NYSED a corrective action plan that detailed what corrective action the district was taking to ensure change within the local school. If the school failed, then the state would declare the school to be in restructuring (Scott, 2009). Under Restructuring, the district was required to select an option which included "reopening the school as a charter school, replacing all or most of the school staff or turning over school operations either to the state or to a private company with a demonstrated record of effectiveness" (USDOE, 2011).

In New York State, New York City and Rochester City School District, along with Hempstead High school (a suburban district on Long Island with a large population of poor minority students), were permitted to take large school buildings and break them apart into smaller school programs that shared the same physical structure (Al-Muslim, 2013; Schwartz et al., 2011).

This action echoed the work of the Bill and Melinda Gates foundation, and other large scale national research organizations and philanthropies that were urging the large urban high schools be phased out for smaller schools (Ravitch, 2016). I have personal experience with these events, as I was a member of the New York State Education Department School Improvement team (Ellis et al., 2011).

As part of these significant restructuring activities, schools under the ARRA act, and then under the Race to the Top initiative received 2,000,000 dollars for three years per new building. This amounted to significant awards of money to these districts with struggling students from the federal government. The federal Race to the Top required that a principal who had been at the building for three or more years be removed, that at least 50 percent of the staff be replaced and that the district support implementation with additional funds. Furthermore, in 2010 the federal government agreed to provide urban schools with Teacher Improvement Fund grants totaling over $40 million dollars (USDOE, 2010). The money was targeted 100 percent for urban schools. The New York State Education Department has structured much of its technical assistance to support the largest urban schools in the state. Besides the frequent reviews conducted by the department under the School Under Registration Review, School in Need of Improvement, Persistently Lowest Achieving and, following the creation of ESSA, Priority Schools, most internal and field-based support capacity at the Department is focused in urban centers. The special education office is given the task of reviewing schools in regions that are based around urban centers. The school improvement team was assigned the large urban districts as their priority (except for Long Island, where small suburban districts in political and fiscal stress received additional support). The curriculum team conducted phone calls with the urban schools on a regular basis and has extremely limited contact with rural schools unless a complaint is made (Jakubowski, 2021).

Finally, the previous governors' own budget clearly demonstrates a lack of concern about rural schools. In a statement made to the press concerning small cities and schools, the governor empathized with their plight during the great recession of 2008–12 but stated clearly "If you are a school district, or a city, or a town or a county, and you are looking for a fundamental financial reform, consolidation is one of the obvious ones" (Gormley, 2013).

The previous governor and the state have placed increased mandated policies on many rural schools. Accountability for test performances is only the beginning, as schools now need to ensure that all teachers are highly qualified. In many instances, these qualifications are specialized, and do not offer rural districts the opportunity to hire generalists. Rather, candidates must be found that are certified to teach multiple subjects within a discipline. Science is the most obvious, as there are different certifications for biology, chemistry, earth science, and physics. The state has increased the number of audits that are required in districts and has begun requesting additional separation of duties in finance that may not be practicable in rural areas.

The final area of state policies includes increased reporting burdens on schools. The state is turning increasingly towards central data gathering, requiring schools to increase the number of hours administration must devote to uploading scores and incident reports. Additionally, there is a movement among the state to require students to take tests on computers via the internet, which rural areas may be lacking in broadband capacity and equipment (Brenner et al., 2020; Vergari, 2009).

Simultaneously, the governor has increased aid to urban schools through special aid packages to urban districts. While schools are nowhere near whole, or even receiving the level of aid required under the Contract for Excellence settlement, rural schools continue to face pressures to shed programs and opportunities for their students, as suburban and urban areas add programs.

RURAL RESPONSE TO LOSS OF EDUCATIONAL AID

In many rural schools in New York, the loss of state aid translates into ending programs. Since New York State has mandatory commencement requirements, many of the smaller schools discontinue electives, including Advanced Placement due to the high cost and low enrollment. In Livingston County, a recent class valedictorian was denied admission to one of the elite state schools due to a lack of Advanced Placement courses (Livingston County News, 2012).

In other areas, schools have curtailed sports programs, once seen as the community lifeblood in many rural areas. In many suburban districts, parents will band together, and re-institute favored sporting programs through a booster club. But rural communities do not have the fiscal wherewithal to accomplish this task. School sports in rural communities may be the only extracurricular activities offered in an area. While in suburban areas, a host of community organizations exist to provide extracurricular offerings the school is seen to adjunct the music, arts, athletics, and social developmental organizations. Because New York State's school tax rate is determined by property values, in rural areas, where wealth is limited, a 1 percent rate increase may only translate into the cost of one teacher, whereas in suburban communities a 1 percent increase is the cost of a new program in arts or athletics (Livingston County News, 2012).

As the *New York Times* reported, many of the cuts in educational aid have been to the poorest communities, which rely the most on state aid. "Overall, cuts to poor and middle-class schools were two to three times larger per pupil than those imposed on wealthy schools" (Easton, 2012). Rural communities react to the decline in state aid by defeating the local budget when the tax rate increases were deemed too high. Since the implementation of the 2 percent tax cap, many rural schools face increasing costs in healthcare and retirement, with limited state aid increases. Under the law, a supermajority of a school's voters must agree to a tax increase over the legal limit if the new budget is enacted. A dire warning for many superintendents exists if the budget is defeated, as the law no longer limits spending to inflation, it now limits the amount that can be collected to the same rate as the previous year (0% levy increase).

Some rural schools are trying to increase the use of BOCES and sharing services. There has been a dramatic uptick in the number of shared services studies conducted by multiple consultant firms. In many locations, the superintendents will declare the studies are not preludes to mergers, but hint that fiscal and educational insolvency is within two years.

BOCES services include the assumption of some functions by the regional cooperative that the local schools handled previously in their own right. Many of the BOCES services are "back room" activities that do not affect the day-to-day operations of the classroom. Typical BOCES service contracts include assumption of business offices and the accounting operations, the bidding on products under a shared contract, including fuel for bus fleets, food products, non-perishables, and cleaning supplies. Other BOCES services include sharing health care plans as a way of reducing overall premiums for districts. BOCES has also assumed the role in creating more shared coaching and instructional leadership services for schools. In some places, the Race to the Top Network teams and Curriculum and instructional support have become cooperative endeavors as changes are rapidly moving beyond the ability of the school principal to lead the instructional changes and manage a building's physical plant simultaneously. With the ending of RTTT funding, and shifts during COVID-19, many districts are now receiving Recovery and Reinvestment funding to close the "performance gap" from losing almost two years of schooling. In my time as an instructor at an upstate college, I found that most of the students in the education department were from Long Island, and did not intend to stay in the upstate region. Finding teachers for rural, and remote schools continues to be a significant problem, especially as state colleges need to recruit tuition-paying students (Jakubowski, 2022; Knipe and Bottrell, 2023). These actions, by policy makers, have created a series of obstacles for rural areas to overcome.

GRIM REALITIES AND NEW HOPES

As the economy of the rural portion of New York State continues its stagnation, more and more school districts will be faced with decisions to reduce programming, or seek outside help (Mueller et al., 2021; Sipple and Yao, 2015). What follows are some examples of how rural communities rethought their educational systems with economic uncertainty heightening the urgency to do something.

In Piseco, and Raquette Lake, New York, in the hills of the Adirondacks, the physical structure of the school exists, the Board of Education still meets, and a superintendent oversees the business operations, but no children attend. Both communities, realizing attendance had fallen to a point that calling school was no longer feasible, decided to tuition their students to neighboring districts. Raquette Lake sends students to Indian Lake and Piseco sends children to Lake Pleasant (Meinxer, 2012). The idea of inter-district transfers by tuition holds promise in many rural areas, especially in New York State. The receiving districts appreciate the children, as well as the additional operating capital to have an increased number of programs, while the sending communities still hold down tax rates, and have hope that someday their school will rebound (Jimerson, 2002).

In Newcomb, also in the Adirondacks, the school was on the verge of shutting down, when the superintendent decided to invite exchange students to the community as a way of bumping enrollment and seeing much needed tuition dollars flow into the school. The superintendent has stated that he feels the exposure of his own students to the exchange students has enlightened them on the competitiveness of world schooling and exposure to communities from across the globe. The superintendent is now advocating for a change in the law in the state that exchange students are limited to one year of education in American schools. Further, the superintendent is seeking permission to build dorms for exchange students who do not wish to live with host families. (Casto, 2012; Winerip, 2011).

In a 2018 report on the status of rural schools in the Southern Tier, the *Olean Times Herald* reported that the continued status was "left behind" (Dinki, 2018). A quote from the report indicates that:

> often struggle to give their students the programs they need in the face of shrinking enrollments and a declining tax base. The two-county area's 24 school districts have lost more than 14 percent of their students over the last decade, which means they get high per-pupil state aid—but the total is just not enough. Taxpayers can only afford to pay for less than a quarter of their budgets. That's a scenario that plays out in many of New York's rural school districts, which account for roughly 300 of the more than 700 districts statewide. "They don't

have any money and they don't have any kids," said Dr. Alan Pole, a retired superintendent who's a consultant to districts across the state, including local ones. "So what's left for the kids in some of these school districts is a real lack of opportunity for their high school careers and to be competitive in college." One measure of opportunity is whether high schools offer Advanced Placement courses or International Baccalaureate diploma courses, which allow students to earn college credit.

But New York's rural schools are the least likely to offer these courses. These realities are difficult, and as the continued socio-economic decline has been cited as a significant barrier to improved community development in rural areas.

One potential solution to the barriers have included a unique, decade-old experiment. The State University of New York-Albany, in cooperation with the Questar III and Capital District BOCES created Tech Valley High School program (P-TECH) that draws students from a 13-county region in Eastern New York State. This program allows students to focus on technology including nanotech, and medical manufacturing that has become a boom industry in the Hudson Valley region of the State. In areas including the finger lakes, western New York, and other population declining areas, legislation is being sought to combine districts into regional high schools. Unfortunately, the State laws do not permit this at the moment (Moon, 2012).

Finally, some schools are sharing superintendents to reduce administrative expenses. Many communities are leery of having an administrator serve two communities, especially considering the increased mandates from the office of state comptroller, teacher evaluation process (APPR), the new curriculum (Common Core), and the required Board of Education meetings. Some of the superintendents believe the job can be done, but it requires the additional increase in other administrator's workloads (Andrews, 2014; Sharp, 2012). The recent Every Student Succeeds Act (Harbatkin, 2022; O' Shea and Zuckerman, 2022) have found recruitment, turnover, and improvement of teachers is often difficult. The lack of professional development opportunities is few and far between for teachers. Principals were concerned with lack of resources, and multiple roles, with limited support, as the small districts are often inadequately represented in policy and funding developments.

With COVID-19 pandemic having dramatically impacted the K-12 and higher education models, some positives did emerge, as the use of digital technologies have created an alternative method for education which may support some rural districts who are seeking innovative programming. Second, the economic hyper acceleration of wage growth, and the ability of professionals to work remotely have created a potential positive for rural areas. Companies who were advantaged in the labor market are suddenly forced to offer increased wages in all areas, as a labor shortage is still underway in the transition between 2022–2023. Rural areas are also seeing a slight increase in populations, as some families are moving to the countryside to establish a "slower pace of life" as Sherman (2021) found as a conflict between residents and newcomers. My own experience (Ellis et al., 2011) of relocating as the initial disruption of the pandemic led me from upstate New York / western New York, to Lower Eastern Shore Maryland.

WHAT SHALL THE FUTURE HOLD?

The global impact of the COVID-19 pandemic will impact schools, and especially rural areas for decades to come. In my personal experience, rural areas in New York have seen since March 2020, several challenges, including early retirements by staff exhausted by pandemic teaching. Support staff in rural schools are leaving the underpaid jobs for greater economic opportunities as competition for labor is finally raising wage rates after decades of artificial suppression. Teacher recruitment concerns continue, as previous economic conditions forced colleges to close teacher education programs.

Within the communities, a sudden skyrocketing of housing values has led to the doubling or tripling of sales prices, and vacant land is especially sought after, as wealthy outsiders are moving beyond traditional areas for second vacation homes. In Otsego County alone, a house which had sat for a decade unsold at a requested price of $80,000 in 2008, is now, in 2022 valued at almost three hundred thousand dollars. With the starting salaries of many rural teachers at the low 40,000-dollar mark, the ability to live in areas without rental property, or buy a house seems beyond reach.

The COVID-19 pandemic also demonstrated how crucial schools are to basics, like food and shelter. The school's extra curriculum, internet access, educational technology, basic medical, and food services were an important part of the program, and crucial for at risk children in the areas. School faculty, staff, administration and volunteers were part of food distribution drives. Bus drivers worked to deliver educational materials and food to residents. In some instances, buses became mobile hotspots for intermittent internet use. This leads me to one conclusion. Infrastructure in many rural areas is not just enhanced by schools, rather the school is the infrastructure in many rural communities.

Chapter 5

State of the State for Rural New York

Schooling rural children in New York State continues to occupy politicians, educational leaders, and local community members. From the provision of tuition to Common Schools (Beadie, 2008) to the desire to deal with the "rural problem" (Biddle and Azano, 2016; Cubberly, 1914; Justice, 2004; Steffes, 2008) government officials have attempted to address challenges that have been faced not only at the state level, but nationwide. Since the turn of the twentieth century, state bureaus of education across the United States have begun to recognize a discrepancy in the educational quality between small rural districts and large urban communities (Azano et al., 2021; Sherman, 2021; Steffes, 2008). The quality of both curriculum and personnel in rural schools has become a particularly contentious factor. The retention of both teachers and administrators (Kamrath, 2022; Leech et al., 2022; McHenry-Sorber and Campbell, 2019; Miller, 2012), coupled with copious academic challenges (Dupere et al., 2019; Howley and Howley, 2010; Jordan et al., 2012; Mykerezi et al., 2014; Piscitello et al., 2022; Tieken and Montgomery, 2021), have caused rural schools to struggle immensely in their ability to provide instruction and educational opportunities that are comparable to what urban and suburban districts are able to offer their students. Critics argue that rural schools are unable to prepare students for a global world and, by extension, that rural school systems do not provide adequate education for students. Because the right to adequate education for all students is guaranteed under the New York State Constitution (Rebell, 2011/2012), a closer examination of the "rural problem" is necessary, especially in terms of relevant policy, economic challenges, sociodemographic patterns, and the potential solution of school consolidation.

THE ECONOMICS OF RURAL SCHOOLS

Available state aid to schools has decreased drastically since September 11, 2001, and because education spending composes a significant percentage of budgets in states, governors are increasingly making efforts to both reduce spending and ensure that states are competitive in order to attract employers and money (Farrie and Sciarra, 2022; Sipple and Yao, 2015; Shober, 2012). The costs associated with educating a rural child are far higher than in an urban environment, which is partially due to the lack of population density (Dhaliwal and Bruno, 2021; Kolbe et al., 2021; Strange, 2011). As schools were named as a primary cause for inflated property tax bills (Schneider and Berkshire, 2020; Suozzi, 2008), which has become burdensome for taxpayers and constituents in rural areas particularly, the Suozzi (2008) and Lundine (2008) Commissions were empaneled by then New York State Governor Eliot Spitzer to identify strategies to reduce the property tax burden (including a reduction in the number of schools and the consolidation of smaller school districts, Lundine, 2008). For many New York taxpayers, the largest portion of their yearly tax bill is their school taxes, and New York workers see one of the highest rates of income taxes in the country as a result of the state utilizing income revenue to transfer money between wealthier urban downstate and poor rural upstate. This presents a problem for rural districts, whose dependency on state aid is higher than wealthier, less financially encumbered suburban areas (Sipple and Yao, 2015).

With the economy slowly coming out of the 2008 Great Recession many rural districts are faced with organizational challenges which have continued almost a decade later. These challenges are further exacerbated by the COVID-19 pandemic (2020–2021). After a decade of significant economic decline, and rising local school taxes, the state enacted a 2 percent growth limit on the tax levy that districts could ask from their population. Coupled with a decrease in state aid and rising employee and support costs, many districts' budgets went into structural deficit. While the COVID-19 relief funding, and continued government expenditures in New York State are "closing a gap" many superintendents are leery that these short-term funding fixes will create, along with rising salaries and other post COVID-19 labor costs, a worsening economic situation in years ahead. Adding to school district's issues, the media has become intensely interested in how public schools are spending public tax dollars, and continue to question decisions concerning compensation, pensions, and health care costs that seem high in such economically depressed areas (NYSSBA, 2014). As demonstrated in my dissertation research (Jakubowski, 2019) local media are especially vigilant of any potential story concerning school district expenditures. Local newspaper editors are interested in promoting school consolidation to cut costs, and create more efficiency and effectiveness, in their opinion, in the public schools within their readership region (Jakubowski, 2019).

The latest challenge is the Critical Race Theory rhetoric, and conservative push back against resources in the classroom (Jakubowski, 2022). While New York is considered a "liberal state" the 2022 midterm election resulted in a small "red wave" in delegations to Washington, DC (Mann, 2022). Citing the 1619 project, and books in the school library, as well as other resources which are objectionable to some conservative residents, interest groups ran candidates for school board seats hoping to promote anti-CRT (Schemmel, 2022). Most of the rural counties in New York State are homogeneous in demographics and viewpoints. The 2020 Census data indicated that the ten most rural counties in New York (Hamilton, Lewis, Essex, Delaware, Chenango, Schohaire, Alleghany, Franklin, St. Lawrence, and Schulyer) were 81.1 percent or higher, white. (Franklin is home to a Mohawk native community, Delaware contains almost 5 percent of Hispanic identifying populations.) The eight most homogeneous populations of the counties are all 90 percent or greater, white. As the *New York Times* reported for the 2022 midterm elections, all 10 counties overwhelmingly voted Republican. With these conservative views, often originating from homogenous populations, local residents often question the role of government, government expenditures, and salaries of public officials. As Cramer (2016) found in her work in Wisconsin, rural residents questioned the perceived high levels of public (and educator) pay and benefits. In my own research (Jakubowski, 2019) I found similar objections in rural New York, and often newspaper editorial questioning of perceived high compensation and benefits packages. The newspapers will utilize editorial decision making, including reporter coverage, and editorials to promote the narrative that local schools in New York State are costly, and need to "do something" to improve their efficiency and effectiveness. In the narrative from local papers, the only solution to these problems is obvious: merge (Jakubowski, 2019). The editors make a connection in their rhetoric to the budget expenditures, and the high tax rates in these rural areas. As such, they connect the high tax rates to population fleeing, and the inability to attract growth. The work of Fischel (2005) utilizes the Tibout theory, or populations of like-minded individuals will tax themselves at a rate to provide desired services. Yet as Sherman (2021) pointed out, often in areas where the population has shifted, newly arrived residents, with greater wealth, and aspirations for their children, desire a higher tax rate in education than the established residents can afford.

Population losses in upstate counties (defined as north of Interstate 84) in New York have become significant and, especially, a source of deep concern (Associated Press, 2012; Churchill, 2023; Upstate United, 2022). Hamilton

County is the most rural county, and smallest by population in the state. The county is projected to lose half of its population within the next twenty years, and many counties have found themselves in similar circumstances. As the rural Catskill region of the state struggles to recover from the aftereffects of Hurricane Irene and a tropical storm, communities are finding that their schools are steadily emptying. Residents are moving out of the area at an increasing rate as rebuilding efforts become stalled by lack of available funds, especially in high tourism-dependent regions. The 2020 census indicated five counties in "upstate New York" experienced population growth: Albany, Saratoga, Schenectady, Tompkins, Yates. The ARC Counties, except for Tompkins, experienced a greater than 4 percent decline in population (McMahon, 2020). One factor that is cited by pundits and media members is the linkage between good schools and the ability to attract and retain new populations.

Multiple studies have examined this relationship between education and mobility out of rural communities, and Davidson (1996) evaluated the increased economic despondency of local communities as a result of this activity. In his work, the communities, and by extension, schools were dying as economic opportunities dissipated and mobile workers with education left to pursue opportunities elsewhere. While many researchers have demonstrated correlations between educational and economic levels of families (Kaushal et al., 2011; Reardon, 2011; Reardon and Robinson, 2008), the correlation between schooling and economic advancement is not always direct in rural communities with high levels of poverty due to the factors associated with outmigration. In fact, researchers (Azano et al., 2019; Carr and Kefalas, 2009; Corbett, 2007; Niccolai et al., 2022; Vazzana and Rudi-Polloshka, 2019) have gone so far as to argue that rural schools actually set up communities for failure by educating different striations of students to leave for "the bigger city." At this rate, struggling rural schools are headed for economic failure, which would certainly preclude them from providing students with an adequate education.

Some recent research has seen changes to the narrative of leaving, and Seelig and McCabe (2021) reported that teachers are staying in rural schools. First, teachers who stay are committed to students. Second, there are often greater opportunities for leadership and collaboration. Third, teachers become connected to the community. Fourth, there are personal and professional ties to the area. The research is bolstered by Gallo (2020) finding rural educators who actively work to change narratives of deficiency, which are often troupe-like, and do not hold value in the narrative. Leech et al. (2022) found similar information, and advanced the notion that rural teacher preparation programs need to be more engaged. As Azano et al. (2021) describe in their work, many teacher preparation programs have not engaged adequately with rural focused preparation. McHenry-Sorber and Campbell (2019) found that in rural areas, the recruitment of rural teachers is a significantly difficult undertaking. The research also found feelings of agency, especially among rural district leaders, was declining, as greater national trends on teacher shortage were hurting recruitment efforts.

INFRASTRUCTURAL BARRIERS FACING RURAL SCHOOLS

In 2006, The Winner Commission undertook a listening tour under the auspices of the "Vision for New York" project. Within the report from the listening tour, the commission cited nine individual priorities in education that must be addressed in order to ensure schools can prepare young rural residents for the future and fulfill their constitutional right for an adequate education. Out of the nine, two of the most important points that the commission identified were the need to "view schools as community centers," and the obligation to "address teacher retention issues" (p. 9). The school as a community center can be defined as the services that are provided to the rural residents at the local school which go beyond traditional educational offerings and include health care, adult employment training, cultural and social events for the local population. Research has found that in rural areas, there is a significant gap in the number of providers for community services mentioned above, and in order to enhance the infrastructure of rural areas, the local school becomes the focal point for service providers in the rural environment (Duncan, 1999; Fitchen, 1991).

Within the Winner Commission's Report (2006) was State Senator Stachowski's remark that "many rural and urban problems are similar" (p. iii). However, contrary to his assertions, urban communities have greater access to and availability of a variety of community-based support resources, such as emergency food supplies, mental and physical health services, and receives much more attention when issues and difficulties arise. Rural schools and communities face a unique set of challenges that are not comparable to the nature of urban and suburban school challenges. Creating such "community centers" out of schools would be a multifaceted undertaking, as many of the most pressing rural issues are academic and economic in nature.

For example, The Rural School and Community Trust gauged rural school's abilities to meet their student's academic needs. In its 2009 report, the Trust found that New York State had one the "critical levels" of district need. They asserted that students in rural New York schools have some of the lowest NAEP scores in the nation. The Trust also specified that New York had the most significantly underperforming rural school system in the country, coinciding with the development of pockets of rural poverty (which is arguably a phenomenon that New York State's economy has enabled). The trust, in subsequent reports, and in conjunction with ARC 2022 data indicate rural New York is economic moribund. One major issue facing many rural communities is the closure of the largest, or single, employer in an area as companies move production overseas. DeYoung (1991); Doukas (2003); Duncan (1999); Fitchen (1991); Sherman and Sage (2011); Sipple et al. (2019); and Thomas (2003) found the closing of a major employer in a community resulted in the loss of employment opportunities and a concurrent drop in the educational attainment of residents in rural communities. Another major issue is the lack of internet broadband, limiting access to the information and commerce exchange networks that dominate the suburban and urban areas (Brenner et al., 2020). Addressing those issues would be necessary in order to reimagine schools as community centers.

In addition to the challenge of conceptualizing schools as community centers, a lack of amenities and occupational comforts has led to the challenge of retaining teachers in rural schools. In many rural schools, teachers have reported a desire to leave due to few retail establishments, entertainment options, and frequent out-of-school interaction with their pupils and the families of their students. These major concerns have led to many teachers gaining experience in a rural setting but leaving for suburban school communities which are typically located in areas with more options for social activities and greater out of work privacy (Greco, 2007; Maranto and Shuls, 2012; White and Reid, 2008).

Many rural teachers have been found to be unprepared and inadequately educated according to recent findings for careers in rural education (Ajayi, 2014; Azano et al., 2021; Barley and Brigham, 2008). To compound the problem, rural schools face difficulty in attracting and retaining teachers that possess minimum teaching credentials, let alone teachers that are experienced and considered to be effective. Science, Mathematics, and technical subjects are increasingly difficult areas in which to recruit and retain teachers in rural districts, especially when private sector employment is, by comparison, better compensated and better equipped to provide high professional growth potential (Greco, 2007; Miller, 2012). In suburban districts, teachers are given an opportunity to specialize in fewer course preparations, a greater range in student abilities in a single classroom and greater professional development opportunities within the school and regional support structures such as BOCES. These factors, which, to an extent, are beyond the control of rural districts, nevertheless continue to be taxing, difficult to resolve, and an obstacle to schools' ability to provide adequate education to all students.

Even though school administrators were not mentioned as one of the nine priorities of the Winner (2006) commission, most research has identified school leaders as a significant factor in teacher retention in rural schools. The efficacy of school leadership affects teacher performance and satisfaction in myriad ways, and rural school teachers may be particularly affected by the challenges faced by their administrators since many are not professionally equipped to navigate rural school climates. In many rural communities, the office of superintendent is marked by frequent turnover, and short tenure. Superintendents cite very specific reasons as to why rural school district leadership is not easy. First and foremost, they feel inadequately trained to perform successfully and address areas of concern in their positions. Many of the programs for school leaders are generic, with very few including preparation for region-specific challenges. Statistically, many superintendents will begin their superintendent assignments in a rural area, and are frequently advised to do so by mentors and other professionals in the field. However, in these rural districts, professionals who have previously focused on instructional tasks will instead be asked to oversee budget, state paperwork requirements, personnel, and other business functions. The superintendents are frequently the only administrator in many very rural schools and are expected to function as the principal; this can often create an overwhelming situation in which there is exceptionally limited support for the administrator. Such constraints not only negatively impact administrators, but teachers as well, and are a contributing factor to low teacher retention rates in rural schools (Abshier et al., 2011; Alsbury, 2008; Canales et al., 2010; Lamkin, 2006; Sansouci, 2007).

Governor Hochul has announced additional funding in 2023 for recruiting teachers. The University at Buffalo has received a multimillion dollar SEED grant from the United States government to increase teacher residencies. The national and regional professional networks are advocating for, and providing clearinghouses for rural teacher recruitment. As Sageman (2022) reported, rural communities, teachers, residents, and others are pushing back on school closure, because it leads to population loss.

RURAL COMMUNITY PUSHBACK

Despite the clear socioeconomic and policy issues, rural schools face yet another challenge in the strife between reform-minded educators, and resistant students, parents, and communities. Historically, frontier and rural areas of the United States have become mythologized as areas of independence and rugged individualism. Lincoln, Jackson, and William Henry Harrison all used frontier, or rural, symbolism in their campaigns for the presidency. Turner's thesis on the closing of the frontier is noted as one of the most significant pieces of research in American historiography. The frontier, or rural, parts of America have been seen by many as a place to go to "start over" and escape urbanization or "the state." This is especially true of the dissatisfaction many rural communities feel when confronted with new mandates from the state or federal government, and such strong, long-standing sentiments have created friction in the face of reform.

The role of parents and community members in reform has been a particularly touchy subject. Woodrum (2004) study examined the nature and degree of parental resistance in a rural community to the introduction of new testing by the state within the school system. A parent remarked that "there was a question on the test that asked something about a wharf. These kids don't know what a wharf is" (p. 4). Many parents regarded test questions and their value and relevance in a similarly apathetic manner, and the study found that most of the test questions and state-mandated curriculum did not reflect the community values or the educational system that parents expected for their students. Teachers within the school discussed the role of schooling as readying children for roles beyond and outside of the community, but parents in the school expressed a desire to establish a direct connection between home and school. One parent lamented: "and they teach them and they go off and live in faraway places. That's not what I want for him" (Woodrum, 2004, p. 6), indicating disconnect between community values and aims of school reform.

These findings are also echoed in Corbett's (2009) study of rural Canadian fishing villages and their education systems, especially at the high school level. The high school period is defined as a time to "buckle down and form an adult identity" (p. 164), and parents expect the schools to equip their children with the skills needed to survive as adults. Further, some parents adamantly refuse to allow their children to become trapped in the fisheries of the local community. They sense the need to "push them out" or allow the "pull of jobs" to help them leave. These parents are concerned that their children will make the wrong choice during a "high stakes decision point" that will prevent choice opportunities for their child. Other parents are glad that their children know that the local resource extraction is their career path because "(he) can't afford to fool around in university for three or four years. That would be a waste to come back with a degree [if he is working in fishing]" (p. 173).

Corbett (2005) further found a low instance of high school graduation rate for the families that stayed close to the home rural coastal village. "The young workers have relatively low levels of formal education, forming an easily exploitable pool for low wage and . . . temporary . . . part time work" (62). Because many of these young men marry and start families at a young age, they tend to work in industries that are labor-intensive and do not place as high a value on education. The children of these young men continue the cycle of resource extraction and entering "family businesses" of fishing. Meanwhile, many of their classmates who do graduate from high school attend colleges and universities in urban areas in other regions and their education enables them to settle away from their community. Two types of educated villagers, however, do return: teachers and business executives employed by local companies. Some women who gained an education also returned to be with family, but many have difficulty finding work directly aligned with their credentialing (Corbett, 2005). Values in rural communities are more often centered on work and labor in the local community than they are in the pursuit of high-quality higher education via a rural diaspora. Some researchers, including Stanley et al. (2008) and Willis (1977) examining roles teachers play in student perceptions of school value found that teachers' involvement can increase students' understanding of school value, attitudes cultivated in the home had the strongest influence.

It is because of such measures of resistance that rural schools have been referred to as places where reforms go to die. This harsh statement primarily emerges from reformers' frustration with the lack of educational improvement despite the distribution and utilization of significant resources in schools. Undoubtedly, the federal government expected to see results from the trillion-dollar investment in high poverty communities, which was meant to be accomplished with the enactment of NCLB. Both parents and teachers, on the other hand, continue to ascertain that "this is what we have always been doing" in the face of new reform efforts. Teachers specifically argue that, in many ways, testing and reform doesn't reflect

> what the real progress is where did that child start and where did that child end. If a child has put for a 100% effort all year long, and they've made gains, and if I [as the teacher] port forth a 100% effort all year long, and that child has made gains, then that's important thing. (Gordon and Patterson, 2008, p. 30–31)

This sentiment is seen across research studies that posit that the teacher will be the ultimate arbitrator of reform movements within their classroom, and principals will serve to buffer their staff from the external winds of change. Buy-in from teachers is essential for reform efforts to have even a chance at successful implementation.

Buy-in is just as necessary from parents. Research studies have shown an intimate interconnection between the rural school and its community; community residents feel especially connected to their schools and obligated to involve themselves in school activity. Adults who work in the school take on an identity as a member of the school and its community, as rural schools' frequent status as the main employer of community members intertwines community members intimately with reform efforts (Peshkin, 1978; Peshkin, 1982; De Young, 1995; Renyolds, 1999). Recent consolidation failures in the Mohawk Valley exemplify the vast importance of the interconnectedness of a rural school and its community, and how that may serve to undermine reform efforts in ways that are not typical of urban and suburban districts in general (Bader, 2012). Cordova and Reynolds (2020) point out, the view point of rural schools as a deficit must end. Place-based education will help in this effort, as well as increased policy initiatives and advocacy. Campbell-Halfaker and Gregor (2021) point out a critical need to honor the ruralness of residents, and ensure that the uniqueness is apparent in work conducted in rural areas. The authors advocate for social justice for rural students, and describe the needs of community, professional, and contextual progress for rural residents.

CAN SCHOOL CONSOLIDATION IMPROVE EDUCATIONAL OPPORTUNITIES?

Research exploring the effects of local school consolidation has indicated that school consolidations do not significantly reduce costs. In many ways, consolidations can increase local expenditures on education (Yinger, 2020). Administrative duplications (such as two superintendents), increased business and support expenses, and overlapping teaching jobs occur, and must be eliminated. After the duplications are eliminated, money is shifted to different funding priorities such as Advanced Placement programs and additional science classes. Now the local community has seen increased programs, and will once merger aid has ended, need to increase the tax levy in order to maintain a new level of services (Adams and Foster, 2002; Bard et al., 2006; Blauwkamp et al., 2011; Brent et al., 2004; Duncombe and Yinger, 2007; Gordon and Knight, 2008; Zimmer et al., 2009).

A hidden cost within the merging process relates to the phenomenon of "leveling up contracts," which occurs when contract provisions from the two previous bargaining units are combined, and the best provisions of salary and fringe benefits are awarded to members of the new bargaining unit. Within leveling up contracts, an additional cause of increased expenditures is the "hold harmless clause" which occurs in the newly bargained agreements in merged schools. This provision keeps previous staffing levels intact for at least three to five years following the merger to ensure that the school's operations are not disrupted too severely by the consolidation (NYSSBA, 2013).

An additional cause of increased expenditures involves the use of building aid granted under consolidation incentives for the purposes of creating new school facilities. These new facilities increase the costs in educating students as the district spends money to engage architects, contractors, and others involved in moving materials between the old school and the new school. Finally, boards of education may decide to increase administrative staff, as an increased number of teachers and students would likely require additional management in order to complete tasks that were previously not necessary, such as student discipline, athletic directors, or curriculum coordination (Duncombe and Yinger, 2007).

Gordon and Knight (2008) found that consolidations increased district revenues and expenditures. Combined local revenue and state aid increased as the schools consolidated. This could be a positive aspect of consolidation if the new revenue is utilized in an efficient manner by increasing student-centered programming. The authors of this study pointed out consolidation or regionalization did not actually increase efficiency. Efficiency in school finance is defined as the utilization of economic resources without redundancies or waste. One of the specific goals for consolidation is enhanced efficiency in district operations, but the research indicates the process of consolidation does not necessarily allow this goal to be met. The newly formed district may not feel the urgency to reduce wasteful spending by eliminating duplicative staff or redundant buildings, as the increased aid provides a cushion to the district's operating budget. This scenario demonstrates how easily adult self-interest may trump the best interests of students and schools, further reducing the likelihood that the education students are receiving is truly consistent with constitutional requirements.

As research continually demonstrates that rural school finances will likely not be improved by district consolidation, the more salient goal of consolidation would logically be program and curriculum enhancement. Most rural students have been repeatedly found not to have access to high quality, standards-based educational offerings. Since the inception of NCLB, many rural schools have not made Adequate Yearly Progress or AYP, the measure of how well a school is performing against state benchmarks (Farmer et al., 2006). Clearly at a disadvantage, rural students need high-quality programming, curriculum, and resources in order to move towards levels of achievement comparable to their suburban and urban counterparts.

Research into program enhancement after school consolidation is mixed. One study found that students enjoyed the post-consolidated school and found increased learning opportunities waiting for them in the larger district. One participant in the study stated, "I don't remember having AP in my old district, but over here we do." Other students mentioned that the new schools "offer more computer classes and more Family and Consumer Science classes." These quotes indicated the students appreciated the new curriculum offered in their school, and teachers echoed the sentiments as well: "It's much stronger. They offer more . . . Even in junior high, there is more offered." A second teacher commented, "last year we offered AP Calculus and we would not have been able to offer that [in our old school]." Teachers were unanimously pleased with the reduction in preparations, increased professional development opportunities, and meeting and collaborating with new faculty members.

Self (2001a) surveyed teachers eight years after a consolidation of two districts in Ohio. The first survey question asked respondents if they felt they had grown professionally. Nine of the thirteen teachers responded positively. According to Self (2001b), "One of the biggest advantages reported was the fact that teachers have more peers to share ideas with than before" (p. 12). The school community was surveyed, and the majority reported "that increased activities available to students through extracurricular activities were a big advantage of the consolidation" (p. 13). The study found students benefited academically from the merger. It found an increase of 12 additional course offerings over the maximum offered by one of the predecessor districts at the high school level. Overall, the community and stakeholders felt the merger was a success as students and the community benefited from additional core curricular and extracurricular offerings.

A national survey of superintendents conducted by Alsbury and Shaw (2005) who had experienced consolidation reported on 11 findings. Some of those findings indicated that school districts which experienced consolidation saw:

1. broadened and enriched curriculum and programming
2. increased offerings of activities with increase competition
3. expanded socioeconomic and racial diversity
4. greater support resources, and others

The belief that students have benefited from increased socioeconomic and racial diversity is especially enlightening, considering the number of studies that have indicated that mergers tend to fail in communities that are too racially and/or socioeconomically diverse (Peshkin, 1978; Renyolds, 1999).

Despite such positive results, Nitta et al. (2010) reported negative results of school mergers. In one, a principal of a post-merger district indicated the cuts from the merger led to "our class sizes [becoming] larger" (p. 12). Teachers reported that "the classes have gotten bigger, and it's harder to ask questions [to the class]" (p. 12). A second teacher indicated "before we were able to devote more time to our smaller classes than we are to each student in our larger classes" (p. 12). Additionally, some teachers felt the loss of their own school ranked like a "death in the family" (p. 12). These school personnel feelings have the capability to negatively influence post-merger district culture, thereby undermining the goal of raising student achievement within both communities (Nitta et al., 2010).

Using data from 1930–1970, Berry and West (2008) find the increasing size of schools has led to a decrease in student income earnings over their lifetime. The authors report that "The study found evidence that students from states with smaller schools obtained higher returns to education and completed more years of schooling" (p. 24). The authors further point out that "the results indicate that some combination of larger districts and smaller schools provides the greatest return for students, policymakers have historically not followed such a recipe" (p. 24).

Small rural districts face immense struggles in meeting the NCLB AYP requirements. Some policymakers have proposed consolidations to enhance program offerings to students in order to meet increased AYP performance measures. The research to this point has been mixed, with some studies supporting the role consolidation plays in enhancing curriculum, while others have found student achievement decreases when school size increases. When rural students are not afforded access to high quality curriculum, they are unable to compete in the global economy alongside their better-prepared rivals. This, in turn, calls into question whether the state is meeting its constitutional mandate to provide students with a "sound basic education."

Sherman and Schafft (2022) provided a contextualization for changing communities, and how the dynamic between newcomers and long-standing residents can become problematic. One such change, gentrification and development, creates a bifurcation between newly arrived residents, who see the schools as a social mobility aspect to their children's future, and long-term residents who feel increasingly excluded. The ideas brought forth by many relocated individuals often include a bigger is better mentality, urban normative understandings of schooling, and an activism for consolidation as a silver bullet.

CONSOLIDATION IS PROBABLY NOT THE "SILVER BULLET"

Rural school consolidation is not a solution for all states. Each district faces its own unique circumstances with a variety of factors that may impact its ability to provide a "sound basic education" to the students in its care. These factors, ranging from political to economic to infrastructural and community, create a certain climate and culture within a district, and may impede the success of a merger with another district whose own climate and culture may be wrought with challenges. The potential level of the success of a rural school merger is largely situation-dependent, and far from a one-size-fits-all solution.

However, consolidations that are thoughtfully undertaken, with students,' teachers,' school leaders,' and community members' best interests in mind, can be successful. Rural students, in order to meet challenges of a globalized economy, must have access to increased curriculum offerings that are on par with their peers from urban and suburban areas, not only to meet accountability measures, but to be successful in all future endeavors (particularly, career and postsecondary pursuits). Further, districts must make sure sentimentality does not take priority over providing educational opportunities. Successful consolidations require thoughtful planning, dedicated community oversight, and professional investment in ensuring that a "sound basic education" is not only met but exceeded to ensure students are given an education designed for a global economy.

In the Leatherstocking region of New York, a recent attempt at consolidation failed. The two districts were, as part of the Master Plan for School District Reorganization, supposed to consolidate as far back as 1947. In 2019, facing extreme budgetary issues, one district approached its two neighbors to begin a reorganization. A preliminary report examined implementing a three-way centralization of the at-risk district and its two neighbors. The study found that a merger with one district would be more feasible economically, and recommended that due to significant tax rate differences, only one district should be invited to the study.

As the two community school districts explored consolidation, the reports from consulting agencies found that indeed, the attempt made sense. The group recommended that the two districts pursue "annexation" or the dis-incorporation of the fiscally distressed district and its absorption into the more stable district. The local media, and the original school boards were in favor of the consolidation. Signs along the major highway demonstrated that some houses and businesses were pro consolidation. The two schools agreed to share sports and extracurricular opportunities, and jointly host events for the foreseeable future. Then, however, the COVID-19 pandemic struck. In a school board election following the pandemic, in May of 2021, new members of the board of education in the fiscally distressed district were elected. The new board members ran on opposing annexation and wanted the district to solve the fiscal issues internally. These new members cited the loss of autonomy, potentially increased taxes, lost opportunity for "their" students, and hinted that the administration and previous board had somehow mismanaged the district.

In the fall of 2021, the straw vote passed both communities. But opposition in the economically distressed district began to appear in letters to the newspaper, and in the presence of "VOTE NO" signs. An unscientific (I drove the route three days a week) count along the major highway that ran between the two communities and three smaller hamlets, showed that by December 1, 2021, the day of the binding vote, 10 signs were present in the two communities in support of the merger, and nine showed opposition.

The merger passed overwhelmingly in the district that was not distressed. In the economically depressed district, the consolidation attempt was soundly defeated. Using social media (Facebook) I saw that many people who indicated they voted no on the ballot believed that the community had a long history, and a proud tradition, and that it must be maintained. They wanted to keep their identity, but also indicated another, deeper issue: the naysayers started using language of "fake news" to describe the official reports that the district was indeed in economic difficulties. One individual on Facebook indicated that the school officials had "spent us into the problem" and believed that the district had paid its employees too generously. A second person indicated that the district had to do more internally before seeking such a radical solution. Third, another person indicated that the educational program in the district was fine, and federal and state COVID-19 aid postponed the dire fiscal cliff, so the district should have time and resources to reform itself.

As I was examining this attempt at consolidation, I reflected on my dissertation research (Jakubowski, 2019) on a similar district consolidation which failed. So many predictive variables had lined up for the community to implement consolidation, yet it failed. There was a crisis, or focusing event (Kingdon, 2011). The three streams of problem, policy, politics, seemed to align into a "window." One district had exhausted its financial resources. It needed help from its neighboring district. The superintendents, and until the 2021 board election mid COVID-19, the boards agreed that an annexation was the only solution. Yet, following the election in the distressed community, the politics stream ended.

In thinking broadly about how to help rural schools, especially when the endorsed policy of consolidation/reorganization wasn't working, I stumbled across the concept of a "wicked problem" (Corbett and Tinkham, 2014; Farley et al., 2019). Defined as an issue where there is no easy answer, a "wicked problem" defies policy solutions, and is a circular, and often repeated point of conflict between various stakeholders. In Corbett and Tinkham's (2014) evaluation of rural education, they find that rural schools and their problems are "wicked" and defy easy solutions. In rural Canada, boards of education were exacting on separating educational questions and community development questions. Farley et al. (2019) describe how educational leadership preparation needs to address the challenges school systems and their employees will face as they are inherently confronted with wicked problems. The wick problems of rural education are especially acute, as teacher recruitment, and retention, are intersecting with administrative turnover, and are compounded by population declines, and continued disinvestment. As I discussed in a critique of recent research into rural higher education, the enacted curriculum for many education schools is rural located, but not rural serving (Jakubowski, 2022) and as Azano et al. (2021) have pointed out, in alignment the work of Parton (2023); Walker-Gibbs et al. (2018), the movement of rural originating pre-service teachers becomes a significant barrier to returning to home when the programs are urban normative or metro centered.

As Corbett and Tinkham point out, there are real systematic issues in rural education:

> Maintaining boundaries between educational questions (i.e. system questions) and these broader concerns is a way for school boards to protect their territory. It is also a way to legitimize their decision-making process through an agenda concerned with providing services to the individual child whose interests are drawn into system discourse. This focus on individual rights is the neoliberal strategy for lifting school and other public policy debates out of the messy processes of social development and political questions. (Corbett and Tinkham, p. 690)

This is a profound, and in some ways prescient insight into how different socio economic groups, or as Sherman (2021) points out, arrivals, view the local school. The elite or leaders, such as the board of education, administrators, and state policy officials view the school as an *educational* endeavor, separate from the development and improvement aspects of the situated community (McHenry-Sorber and Sutherland, 2020; Sutherland et al., 2022). This often creates dissonance in describing the role of the school for a community. In community member's "nonprofessional" view of the school, it is a crucial part of the community, significantly crucial to community renewal and recovery (Bernsen et al., 2022). As Zuckerman (2019) found in a crucial and innovative study, community members, and professionals in other community development professionals view the school as a central and critical resource to community change and enhancement. The conflict which is presented in the concept of a "Wicked Problem" and the idea by professionals that a school is just a school flies in direct opposition to community development research. In a follow up study (Zuckerman, 2022) found that the communities, the service providers, and the leadership needed to create consensus on how the educational infrastructure would support other collaborative efforts to create development opportunities.

Consolidation, mergers, or reorganizations are clearly an urban normative approach (Fulkerson and Thomas, 2019) to rural problems. Bigger is not better, and efficiency at the expense of local control is a real sticking point for successful centralizing districts. What is further, as Ellis et al. (2011) discuss, there are alignments between my own history and what happened in rural communities in the late 2010s and early 2020s. I witnessed the anger. I saw the distress at the idea that a centralization/annexation/merger may lead to the smaller school closing. And the fears became reality. The policy of the 1950s should be retired to promote significantly more collaboration between communities. As urban reformers often state: a zip code should not limit the educational opportunities of a child.

CONCLUSION

Rural schools are facing significant socio economic, financial, and infrastructural crises. While New York State's constitution clearly requires that all children receive a "sound basic education," current political and economic conditions have largely prevented rural districts from meeting that requirement. Faced with increasing mandates, decreasing resources, and heightened public scrutiny, school systems are struggling to allow for all children to be afforded their constitutional rights. A combination of school finance challenges, community beliefs, and the inability to adequately recruit and retain school staff have created a perfect storm of difficulties for rural schools in the state. While consolidation may be viewed as an easy, seemingly convenient solution to the "rural problem," the process and implementation of consolidations are long, difficult, and do not always produce the desired results. The pressure to consolidate rural schools in New York State has been largely impeded by community members who want to hold on to their identities that have been formed around schools. New York will need to examine the results of its political and economic decisions that may have exacerbated the "rural problem" and seek alternative strategies to ensure that all children receive a competitive education in the future. The continued focus of rural schools and its role in the community is a "Wicked Problem" which requires further research and practitioner discussion.

Chapter 6

The Decayed Community

Losing Schools in Rural New York State

In rural, upstate New York, the area defined as the Catskills and north, a trend continues that Fitchen (1991) described as an ever-increasing out-migration of young students seeking their fortunes and livelihoods elsewhere. The Appalachian Regional Commission (2020) confirmed the data on outmigration. The 2020 census proved that the majority of upstate counties (except for 5) lost 4 percent or more of their populations between 2010–2019. Carr and Kefalas (2009); Corbett (2007); Weis (1990), and others have all described in some detail how communities are increasingly impacted by globalization. Schafft and Jackson (2010) demonstrate how this mobility is increasingly throwing rural communities off kilter and destroying the social bonds that makes what Theobald (2017) describes as the "quaint image of small-town Americana." This chapter examines three instances of a community losing their school after a consolidation. What was the impact of losing the school? This chapter uses first person experience (Ellis et al., 2011; Jakubowski, 2020a; Jakubowski, 2021) materials from the internet and mainstream media, and additional research to provide examples. It is also based on dissertation (Jakubowski, 2019) research into rural areas.

In many communities following a consolidation, one or more schools are closed as part of the reorganization process. Scholars such as Ewing and Green (2022); Miller (2021); Lyson (2002); Thomas (2003); Theobald (1997); Tieken and Auldridge-Reveles (2019); and Sipple et al. (2019) have defined a school as the heart of a rural community. In many instances, the research conducted by those authors tell of rural communities dying after their schools closed. In three selected case studies (Stake, 1995), the community which lost its school after a consolidation lost some of its cohesion. By examining these selected examples, I hope to document in an urban normative (Fulkerson and Thomas) state additional examples of unseen implications of consolidation to rural communities. As part of my own experiences (Ellis et al., 2011) I personally witnessed what happens to areas when the school buildings are closed, and the people are moved elsewhere.

BACKGROUND

New York was selected due to its uniqueness as an urban centered state with significant rural areas. New York, as a state, has promoted a policy of school district consolidation for almost 100 years. But legislatively the state has not mandated consolidation. It has left the decision to consolidate up to the local communities under a "home rule" concept. The *New York Times* is often considered the premier media outlet in the United States. As such, many articles which appear in its pages carry weight with national policy makers. The *Times* has discussed the role of rural schools nationally and within the state in the past decade. These factors give researchers a unique case study area for review. In this current age of government efficiency, multiple states are forcing small rural schools to consolidate to bring down costs, increase educational offerings, and control tax rates. Maine (Lee et al., 2016); Illinois (Gordon, 2015); Kansas (Foster, 2015); and Vermont (Rodgers et al., 2014) are just some of the states actively seeking the policy solution of rural school consolidation to address the problem of budgetary constraints at the state level. In examining the reports and research out of those states, New York State is cited as a source for state level policy makers looking for models of consolidation, and the positives and negatives which emerge from state-level actions. According to NCES (2021) data, New York contains nearly 700 districts, with 324 classified as rural. Charter schools, special act schools, and other educational organizations listed on NCES (2021) as "Local Education Agencies" were included. With around 45 percent of the LEAs in New York State classified by the federal government as rural, New York provides a case study for scholars who wish to examine rural school policy in states which are regarded as "metro" in nature (Fulkerson and Thomas, 2019).

In New York State, the education department leads the school district reorganization process with the help of a local representative of the Commissioner of Education, titled as a District Superintendent. SED and the District Superintendent, along with the local school superintendents and boards of education will guide the self-study process utilizing consultants who are former district administrators. The process usually takes about two years from initial proposal to final completion. It is a long, complex process that contains several complex steps (Chabe, 2011; Tangorra, 2013). Most consolidation efforts in the period under review, defined as 1995–2022 have failed. Usually, identity and community cohesion are cited for the failure to consolidate the smaller, rural districts (NYSABO, 2014). As Sipple et al.

(2019) pointed out, many communities gain economic benefit from a nearby school, including more local services and business opportunities. In districts which have closed a school, the economic impact was present, and negative (Sipple et al., 2019).

Rural schools have been identified as an important element to rural communities. DeYoung (1995); Goodlad (2004); Miller (2021); Peshkin (1982); Reynolds (1999); Schmuck and Schmuck (1992); Tieken (2014), and others have established clearly that a rural school is the epicenter of its community. Tieken (2014) depicts the intimate connection between schools and their community in a first-person narrative fashion. The research clearly shows how the community, and their school are interconnected. In fact, many sports movies and programs including *Hoosiers*, and *Varsity Blues* use the plotline of school athletics as the glue that holds rural communities together. In those feature films, the town is captivated by a sports team in the middle of an athletic season heading towards a state championship. The local school may also be the meeting place for after school activities such as band, theater, scouts, or church groups in the area. Most of the residents within the area attended the school or had family members in the school.

In my personal experience (Ellis et al., 2011), driving around the rural areas of the state, one is almost always greeted by a welcome sign that lists the state championships that the local school has won. In one community that I spent a significant amount of my career in, the athletic teams won state championships in multiple sports. Basketball and football games attracted large crowds, as the community supported the teams in their championship seasons. The local communities that I have called home have been devastated by floods and economic depression in the last 10 years. They rely heavily on outside communities for their very existence (Thomas, 2003). As Sherman (2021) pointed out shifting economies of tourism create a new image in communities moving from resource extraction to bedroom and tourism. This shift has created economic insecurity.

The local school is also the most tangible form of government in many areas (Parshall, 2023; Tracy, 2010). The school board serves as the representative for the people dealing with the education of their children. In New York, the school is the largest percentage of a taxpayer's bill (Tuttle, 2015). In 2022, the Tax Foundation found New York state ranked 50th (worst) for local property tax burden. The State imposed a property tax levy limit, and provided reimbursement for local tax levies, always imposed by the elected board of education leadership. Usually, local tax levies are used to cover the differences between state and federal aid to districts and their total operating expenditures. In Pugh's (1994) study of a school consolidation in New York, the close examination of school boards revealed the interconnectedness of school governance and the community's leadership. Corbett (2015); Howley and Howley (2015); and Theobald and Wood (2010) demonstrate the influence local schools can have on reclaiming their roles as place-based education establishments which can improve community vibrancy.

PUSHING FOR CONSOLIDATION

Discussions about rural education have been a staple of educational policy making for almost 100 years. Biddle and Azano (2016) explore the history of "the rural school problem" in policy discussions. Scribner (2016) examines the history of school consolidation, starting in the early 1900s with the centralization of rural districts and ending with the 2000s and the drive to consolidate school districts. Haller and Monk (1988) found rural school consolidation has a long history in educational policy circles. They found in New York State three distinct phases of consolidation. The first phase combined one-room schoolhouses. The second phase combined village union free districts with rural schools to form centralized school districts and newly constructed physical plants. The third phase was consolidation for efficiency during economic crises of the 1970s and 1980s. Additionally, Parkerson and Parkerson (2015) examined the history of the consolidation movement, which started as an attempt to assert state control over schools through efficiency and increased professionalization in the workforce. The goals of school consolidation continued to triumph the efficiency aspect but added program enhancement as a logical reason to increase school sizes.

Since 2010, there has been an increased desire to consolidate smaller rural districts to fulfill the last three governors of New York's goal of reducing government size and taxes in upstate New York (Lundine, 2008; Winner, 2006; Suozzi, 2008). Governors and past Commissioners of Education have publicly called for the consolidation of small, state aid dependent schools in different venues (Gormley, 2013; King, 2012). Contrary to past practice, the state has indicated additional operating aid would not be forthcoming. School districts would need to reduce spending or merge. Echoing the first Commissioner of Education, Andrew Solan Draper, a proponent of rural school reorganization (Loveland, 1993), Commissioner John B. King, Jr. stated the current system of school governance was not practical for efficient administration (King, 2012). The State Education Department has encouraged rural districts to merge through a 40 percent increase in state aid (Timbs, 1997). The additional aid would help struggling schools facing educational and fiscal bankruptcy keep programs intact, or restore lost ones cut as operating expenses increased and aid and taxes did not keep pace. Yet many communities have not taken up this "free money" because the price of losing their school is too great.

One major hurdle to school mergers/consolidations is the loss of the physical school within the community. In some places, a "gentleman's agreement" is reached to keep the school open in the area until such time as a new structure can be built. In many places, the new district will vote to close the smaller of the schools as enrollment declines, budgets tighten, or additional work is required to upgrade the facility (Enberg et al., 2011). The school building is a representation of the area's spirit. The physical space is a shared experience for the residents of the community (Zimmerman, 2009).

In three recent instances, closing the physical school building after a consolidation created significant community concern, as the elementary schools that were closed are treated not only as the educational center of the area, but the social center as well. The school carries the identity of the community and gives a sense of place for people who anchor memories of childhood to the school and its physical structure. The three examples below were selected from the last twenty years from a northeastern state. The examples were selected due to three major factors. First, the merger studies had assured the smaller community that their school would be maintained following the consolidation of the school districts. Second, each of the communities selected had been part of previously unsuccessful consolidation discussions. Third, I am familiar with the individual circumstances of the districts and was able to follow the discussions using local media sources.[1] The three case studies under review represent the fears expressed by many opponents to school district consolidation. The community will lose their school. With the loss of the physical structure, the residents fear the village itself will disappear. National research demonstrates these fears. Tieken (2014), as one example, expresses the concerns of Delight, Arkansas, residents if the local school closes.

ANNEXATION AND CLOSURE

The first instance of a building closing following a consolidation is the Magical Mountains Central School District. This district, now part of the Uplands-Magical Mountains Central School District, was created out of the annexation of the smaller (250 students) Magical Mountains to the larger Upland Central School District. The Magical Mountains campus was to be maintained as an elementary school for the community according to the consolidation study. It is an old Works Progress Administration era building that has had additions added over the years. It sits prominently on Main Street, defining the transition between the residential areas of the village and the business/government section of the area. While the facility was much loved, there were some serious issues with the campus. The first concern was space. The building was maximized in terms of space. Second, there was no room around the campus to expand. The sports fields were outside of town. The gym was designed for an elementary school, with little space for a high school. The cafeteria usage drove the class schedule, including an interrupted block where children entered class for sixty minutes and then left for lunch, with a resumption of a twelve-minute end of class after lunch.

The Magical Mountain community had a history of pride in its school, and after the initial centralizations in the 1930s and 1940s, had frequently been part of consolidation discussions for over forty years. In many instances, the community had rejected the consolidation proposals by wide margins. The community would rally to keep their school open through protests, letter writing campaigns, and electing board of education members to support the school. In other instances, the other school rejected the consolidations. Some of the rejections were due to the potential raising of taxes if the merger went through. In almost every instance, the consolidation plans maintained a necessity of maintaining the Magical Mountain School as an integral part of the consolidation proposals. With the annexation and then subsequent closure of the Magical Mountain campus, the community felt betrayed and angered. The superintendent of the school district indicated that "With a heavy heart and a lot of anxiety on some of the board members, I think, and parts of the community, yes, we made the decision to bring all of our students here on the Cattaraugus campus and to be one school" (Highland Press, 2012). Many spoke in the local paper about their sense of loss at the closing of the school. Other speakers felt the Magical Mountain community would lose its social cohesion and its feel as a close-knit place to live. One such resident, when one room of the community center was turned into a museum about the school stated: "This is where the history of the school happened . . . To have it back in the school is a double-edged sword. We get to have it back in the school because it's no longer a school."

ECONOMIC REALITY AND LOSS

When the two small communities of Mountainside and Creekside merged in the 1990s, the newly formed board of education agreed to keep the former Creekside Central School district's building open as a working, operational school. Neighboring community members recalled how "One committee member noted that Mountainside and Creekside schools merged in 2004 with the understanding the Creekside building would become the middle school." The secondary, grade 7–12 students would join their Mountainside classmates at the Mountainside campus. The schools are only 10 miles apart in the southern tier of New York State. Rasmussen (2009) describes the region as a series of hills interspersed by valleys created by glaciers in the Stone Age.

The two schools suffered from the economic downturn which affected rural America in the early 2000s. Later, as the Great Recession hit rural schools again, the school district looked to close the smaller building. Calling in a consultant to advise the district, one of the findings was "one of our concerns, really, is what happens to the Creekside community if you close the building." Members of the consulting firms, which advocates for rural education in the state had recognized the economic downturn of the late 2000s, and the failure of the state to offer additional aid, created a major issue for rural schools and communities. "It's not ideal," said the consultant, "but sometimes you have to make difficult decisions." When the building was finally closed, it added to a growing concern in rural areas: what to do with vacant municipal buildings. As one media source reported the superintendent of the district believes "is realistically unsellable. Dozens of empty municipal buildings throughout rural upstate New York have been empty for years, he said." As economic reality of the Great Recession, and Upstate New York's economic crisis solidifies, communities are finding themselves unable to re-utilize old schools. One media outlet revealed that "[c]urrently dismal real estate markets make selling vacant public structures more difficult," superintendent of schools said. The middle school is the largest building in Creekside, a town with a 2010 population of 793 persons. In the Hudson Valley Region of New York, a report indicated that the school aged populations would continue to decline, and more communities would face the challenge of reusing old schools (Patterns for Progress, 2012). One media report indicated that "Virtually all Creekside businesses, on the other hand, are closed. The former Creekside School is nine miles from Mountainside Village." This means the former school building is too far away to be utilized by the only economy left standing.

THE STATE'S ANGER

The third example, from a severely economically depressed area of the Northeast, created such a significant problem the state comptroller found malfeasance following the merger's conclusion. When three school districts merged into one school district, the community approved a bond for constructing a large campus high school. Sometimes, following a merger, the communities agree to a new school building. New York State will provide up to 95 percent reimbursement to the local community when it builds a new centrally located school. In this instance, the new school building was less a temple to education, and instead a house of horrors. The Works Progress Administration schools that had housed K-12 campuses in the three previously independent school districts had been much loved and well cared for.

In the years leading up to the consolidation of the Timberline School District, the Conjunction school district invested heavily in a rehabilitation project on their school. The debt was still there when the three school districts merged. In the newly formed Timberline school district, the outlying community experienced social loss, economic loss, and a sense of anger at the closing of their schools and their sales. The added burden of fiscal mismanagement the state comptroller discovered in its audit of the new school district increased the anger residents felt towards the process. Two such citizens filed an appeal to the Commissioner of Education requesting the decision to close the two schools be overturned (Appeal to Commissioner, 15,318). While the Commissioner did not overturn the decision, this action on the part of two residents should be seen as an extreme measure of protest against the local board of education decision.

The Office of State Comptroller found significant cost overruns in constructing the new campus for Timberline Central school district. In the comptroller's report, the state questioned the spending choices made in building the new school. "The Division's audit disclosed that district officials failed to adopt a comprehensive strategic plan for the merger of three separate school districts into one, consequently mismanaged the merger, and wasted $12.5 million of taxpayer dollars" (OSC, 2006). Further, a review of the consolidation found the overstatement of the potential cost savings associated with the consolidation. Last, the new school district overcharged the communities with a significantly higher than necessary tax levy. The reports found the communities did not benefit from consolidation.

Rather, the closing of two elementary schools decreased the level of community cohesion in the outlying villages. One local media source reported that "The move has sparked protests throughout western Timberline Central School, particularly from residents concerned about long bus rides to the other building." In the new school district, infighting between the board and the administration has caused turnover. The leadership of the school district is looked upon by the community as outsiders who do not have the best interest of their children in mind. As one media source reported: "Still, critics of the school closings say the board should have formed a committee." One respondent was adamant: "Absolutely, said a community resident. She sat on the community budget committee that narrowly voted to keep the schools open." The district administration, following one interpretation of New York State Education law, chose to close the two outlying schools without forming a citizen's advisory committee. Later, as the buildings were put up for sale by the Timberline Central School District, residents protested who was trying to purchase the buildings:

"Members of the school board argued that they had a fiduciary responsibility to the district to accept the highest offer, but some residents did not necessarily agree that was the case, and several residents . . . filed a lawsuit against the school district over what they considered to be irregularities in the proposed sale." According to the media accounts, the people lost trust in the district administration to do what was right for the communities.

LESSONS TO LEARN

What are the lessons that have emerged from the decaying schools in Upstate New York? There are three that merit discussion. Each lesson can find its way into administrators and politicians' considerations of consolidation.

First, the consolidation process, advocated by state leadership, has been resisted in some local communities. For schools in dire fiscal straits, the administration and the community may hold a different viewpoint on what constitutes a dire situation. Administrators and board of education members may find themselves in a struggle against the local community's view of the district's situation (Rey, 2014). Rural communities have heard "the sky is falling" too many times to approve a consolidation study if there are other alternatives available. Local boards and administration should instruct the consultants involved in the consolidation process to explore all alternatives before proposing a consolidation plan.

Second, a local community that agrees to a consolidation that will keep its school open should be prepared for the building's closure through the consolidation process. The disposition of the smaller building should be discussed in the consolidation plan. The community will continue to need community space, so partnerships or shared space agreements with business incubators should be explored. Repurposing older industrial buildings in urban areas is receiving funding boosts. Rural areas should benefit from the infrastructure the retired school can provide. Part of the retired building should become a local historical museum that prominently displays the community's history from the school. Tieken (2014), shows how the school building and its history is key in many villages' identity. That history should be honored through a well-maintained historical society.

The third lesson is one of trust and truth. Rural community residents are inherently distrustful of people who are there to tell the community differently. Peshkin (1982) in his seminal study of rural school communities reminds us that the rural school communities seek to lead and run the schools in their communities with local values in mind. If outsiders, or insiders, are not completely truthful in the process, and do not engage in transparency, then the entire community will shatter and the level of trust in the local school leadership will be destroyed. The concept of a consolidation study is adversarial to begin with. No matter what the study question is, the local community hears: "Why haven't we been doing enough to help our kids?" In groups of people that pride themselves on self-sufficiency, this is a damning self-reflective undertaking. As Evans (1996) found in his research into school change, people identify with a situation, and hold personal identity with the events, even if the results are less than perfect. As Cramer (2016) and my own dissertation (2019) discovered, trust in the state has decreased significantly, and Jacobs and Munis (2022) found, rural residents identify the government as a major source of problems, and do not trust the metro centric, urban normative governments to do right (Fulkerson and Thomas, 2019). Churchill (2023) captured the "upstate" feeling that New York's government continues to favor the downstate region, and encapsulates my experiences with the resentment expressed in rural areas (Ellis et al., 2011).

CONCLUSION

As New York and other states continues to seek ways to improve efficiency in education through the tacit or active support for school consolidation, it should keep in mind the following:

First, residents in rural communities have long memories. They do not forget when school administrators promise to keep a school open as part of a consolidation discussion. The honesty of school administrators is often questioned by rural residents leery of broken promises. If district officials believe that closing one of the schools will improve future potential outlook, it should be addressed in the consolidation study. The studies should address and formalize the expectations, rights, and understandings of community members, professional education administrators, and elected citizens.

Second, the state needs to consider the economic impact of a rural school's closure on a community. The rural areas of New York State do not have the infrastructure or capacity economically to deal with a closed building of a school's size. The state may wish to consider funding innovation hubs, senior citizen housing, or enhanced sites for job placement development. The schools are structured for a learning/living environment. The ability to start boutique business and allow owners to live on site would help jumpstart struggling economies. Richard Florida, in *The Rise of the Creative Class* uses cities as examples of dynamic spaces. Why not rural areas?

Third, states need to provide easier processes for schools to find sharing and cost savings without the "nuclear option" of a merger. Many communities, due to economic reasons, feel pressured into consolidating. There should be steps besides cutting programs and staff and raising taxes before undertaking a consolidation study. Districts may wish to consider sharing core teachers across districts. If shared principals and superintendents are possible, and districts are sharing sports teams, take these ideas further. Schools could look to regionally share music programs, or advanced placement courses. Allowing more freedom to schools academically, with leaner regulations, and a concerted effort to increase state and federal aid to rural areas would eliminate the once a decade Sword of Damocles debate over school consolidations and closures. District leadership could invest the time in developing more supports for students and teachers and the community.

NOTE

1. Names have been changed due to the sensitive nature of the research in rural communities.

Chapter 7

Is New York Unique?

New York is a unique state. For many people, envisioning New York brings forth images of the city or suburbia. But the built-up areas of the state are only one part of this old, historically relevant state in the United States. My own experiences as Ellis et al. (2011) point out in autoethnography, coupled with the Fulkerson and Thomas (2019) urban normative realities have led me to try and capture the uniqueness, and frankly, under-represented nature of non-urban New York. I tried to capture what Kyvig (2019) described as "nearby history" and, with the lack of post–World War II history in *New York History Journal,* and other outlets, create the beginnings of a dialogue.

Home to several powerful, influential, and surviving native peoples, New York has been a central state for many centuries. The area now called New York is *Haudenosaunee* or Iroquois land, composed of a confederacy of five, then six, nations, and several Algonquian groups, the area of now New York was a central point of cultural exchanges, frontier interaction, and conflict, as the *Haudenosaunee* and the *Algonquians* engaged in both competition and collaboration. Today, these influential, and accomplished native peoples live across the state on significantly diminished territory, and across the rest of the United States and neighboring Canada (Hauptman, 2001).

As western Europeans, led by the Dutch, French, and finally the English explored, and then colonized the areas, New York's territory became hot zones of conflict over resources, trade, and access to transportation routes to the north and west. The rivers and Great Lakes, as well as Lake Champlain created the original transportation superhighways (Richter and Merrell, 2010). Today's interstate and federal highways were often imposed upon the original Native people's pathways. After the nation building period of the post–Revolutionary War, and the creation of the Erie canal, New York became the singular pathway, as many immigrants traversed the western route to settle in the mid, and then far west. New York City grew into a transportation and capital hub, while the canal created cities along its banks, and farm villages grew up deeper inland as produce and manufactured goods exchanged from rivers to canals, and then railroads. Smaller cities, at the junctions of railroads and rivers flourished across the state's inland valleys, giving rise to the moniker "The Empire State" (Klein, 2005). Boosterism, small manufacturing plants, and new industries attracted residents into areas deep inland, and New York continued, and then grew, into an agricultural giant in the areas of produce, brewing, and natural resource extraction. This wealth, and civic mindedness, from local entrepreneurs, gave rise to leading arts centers, and educational organizations across the state, far away from New York City.

In the tranquil valleys, and endless mountains, we have colleges, and research universities. Our Appalachian region boasts Cornell University of Ithaca, New York. An Ivy League university with an international reputation, the community of Ithaca, and the surrounding countries benefit from world class research and service. Who can forget Ithaca College, and the artistry and civic engaged graduates of the "other" institution along Cayuga Lake? We also have in our western region St. Bonaventure, which has a basketball history to rival its teacher preparation and community engagement efforts for well over 100 years. We have Elmira College and Mark Twain in the middle part of the state, with the literature, Americana and narrative of the US ingrained in our civic memory. As a proud Bearcat alumnus of Binghamton, the university center is a public institution with a global impact. An incubator, a research hub, and an outstanding education, Binghamton is the place to "B" for many New Yorkers and others. Up Interstate 88, SUNY Oneonta, and Hartwick college are service colleges with amazing programs designed to help civic-minded citizens earn community-engaged degrees. Cortland, home of the New York Jets summer camp for spring, is the home of an outstanding school of education. Who can forget my alma mater, SUNY Fredonia, nurturing intellectuals, artists, musicians, and leaders since its inception in the 1800s? Within New York's southern tier and Catskill mountains are four of our technical colleges, with Cobleskill, Delhi, Alfred, and Morrisville State Tech providing innovative research and critical care for agriculture, technology, and recreation. Our community colleges in the southern tier open pathways to careers, technology, and higher education unlike many other places, benefiting from relationships with businesses who have found homes and headquarters along our natural wonder (Clark et al., 2010).

IBM in Binghamton, Corning, in the Greater Elmira metro, and Amphenol in Sidney are just some of the world-wide companies with presence in the Southern tier. Defense contractors, train, transit, and furniture manufacturing companies all call the rural parts of New York home. We also boast a significant amount of travel, tourism, natural beauty, and agricultural resourcing. The region promotes innovation and centers its work on sustainability towards the environment. The existence of Catskill State Park, the Allegany

State Park, and a number of state forests, and the ban on fracking, while controversial, is environmentally friendly (Simonelli, 2014).

Why am I writing about this area of New York? For starters, Michael Thier, Jessie M. Longhurst, Philip Grant, and Jessica Hocking (2021) recently published a piece in the *Journal of Research in Rural Education* declaring the Northeast a "rural research desert." In my research into rural areas (Jakubowski, 2020b) I found that Upstate New York is not represented well in the national research literature, nor is it considered very rural by niche research areas. New York's rural communities exist at the intersection of a wide range of definitions but are often overshadowed by the urbanity of the state. I also believe that much of the research conducted into rural Appalachian New York is "stuck" in master's thesis, doctoral dissertations, and practitioner work conducted by scholars who morphed into practitioners in school districts, or have moved into a non-scholarly position. I firmly believe that if the voices which spawned the rural identity resentment that Kathy Cramer (2016) talks about in her research in Wisconsin, researchers, journalists, and others must end the deficit model which Biddle, Sutherland and McHenry-Sorber (2019) discuss in their reflection on rural research in the past twenty years. Biddle and Azano (2019) have rightly called out researchers for falling into the trope of rural communities as deficient.

With the 2016 publication of J.D. Vance's polemic, researchers, advocates, and rural community members experienced the frustrating realization that the deficit rural narrative is ingrained in American thinking. As journalists, pundits, and tangential researchers, who have examined sociology, political science, history, and other disciplines without doing the hard work of understanding rural communities continue to fall back on the deficit narrative, the idyllic trope, and the othering of rural America, we forget that spaces like Appalachian New York, and other communities across the United States which pride themselves on rural are great places to live, work, play, and participate. While potentially "preaching to the choir" I hope that this piece begins a dialogue to address what Cervone (2017) and Fulkerson and Thomas (2019) have found, the existence of metro-centered and urban normative discourse in research, policy, and practitioner areas.

What does urban normative, or metro centered mean? Two new words which have emerged recently emphasize an ongoing trend in research. The concept of urban normative can be summarized as the belief that urban existence is the standard. Rural is deficient, different, and not urban. Yet historically, the "rural deficit" narrative hides the reality that up until the urbanization and industrialization of the pre-Civil War through post-World War II era, most Americans lived in rural America. Reformers from different stripes pushed the narrative that urban areas were advanced, and that the school systems were "efficient" and "effective." Rural one and two room schools, and the villages themselves, were too small, too inefficient, and unable to provide an up-to-date education for their children. Even more damning, some of the "reformers" who included Ellwood Cubberley (1914), and Andrew Sloan Draper (Loveland, 1993), the first Commissioner of Education in New York State, and frankly all the Commissioners of Education in New York State, have pushed an unending drumbeat that rural schools are inefficient and ineffective in educating their students to assume their roles in (a metro dominated) society.

After World War II, the leading educational expert of the US Military education system, Francis Trow Spaulding, was appointed Commissioner of Education in New York State. In nearly 11 addresses delivered to a number of groups ranging from the Farm Forum to an essay in the *Ladies Home Journal*, the Commissioner of Education for a state that was (and continues to be heavily rural), indicated that rural children needed to be educated so that "from farms and villages our urban areas replenish their populations and secure manpower for industry and commerce" (Spaulding, 1967, p. 141). In that one line, the Commissioner of Education establishes the roles rural communities are expected to play: human resource recruiting grounds for urban areas. The viewpoints expressed by Spaulding, and the other first five Commissioners of Education cannot be more urban normative or metro centric than the notion rural areas exist, solely, to supply urban areas.

A second reason I write about rural areas in a metro-dominated state are the aftereffects of the January 6, 2021, riots at the US Capitol, and the rise, since the 2016 election of right-winged identity politics and demagoguery. As a research group, with books by Catte (2018); Cramer (2016); Longhurst (2020); and Wuthnow (2018) we cannot say we did not see this coming. There exists in rural America, a significant rage, distrust, and anger against the urban elite, the urban governmental structures, and the urban based reformers which echo in many ways the Populist and Progressive outrage of the turn of the last century. Identity politics, or xenophobia, has taken root, as under employed, and partially disenchanted rural residents see power devolve from their political influences and economic dominance into a "different America" that has different values and different viewpoints than their own.

In three very solidly researched, and profoundly telling works, Cramer (2016); Catte (2018); and Wuthnow (2018) built upon the findings of Duncan (1999) and Reynolds (1999) who found very clearly, rural Americans were increasingly exasperated with "reforms" from urban centers which resulted in losses. Thomas (2003) made clear in his research into the northernmost parts of New York's Appalachia, urban based reforms of schooling, economic policies, and market forces were driving small town America to disaster. In a finely written work which deserves more attention, Doukas (2003) found the people of two communities in New York's northern Appalachian region had given their community over to a major international corporation that frankly acted as a bad corporate citizen. The constant boom and bust within the region, and the continuous threats by the corporate leadership, owned by investment funds based in New York City, created a significant economic decline in a formerly prosperous area. Thomas and Smith (2009) describe the significant division between the mostly rural dominated "upstate" region of New York and the city centric "downstate" area. The flow of taxes, the perception of favoritism in state government, and the allocation of opportunities are all described in the work as a contest between the liberal leaning city voters and everyone else. The contest includes the neocolonial approach New York City has taken to resource allocation, and resource collection. In Thomas' (2005) work, the story of how New York City's water needs literally drowned an entire region is detailed. New York used the "city" and "resident needs" to sink a large section of the Catskills under reservoirs.

The Upstate/Downstate narrative has influenced state policy heavily in the areas of reforms. As I describe (Jakubowski, 2019) educational reformers have pushed for consolidating small rural schools, while openly advocating for large urban schools to break up into smaller units. Parshall (2023) clearly established the push to consolidate small villages has led to conflicts locally. Residents are fearful that by dissolving the village, the empty building and other municipal identifiers will telegraph a death spiral. The State, however, while frustrated with the size and bureaucracy of New York City, pushed other municipalities to dissolve into larger administrative units. The city, however, is not one entity, but rather New York is composed of five boroughs and is the end result of the 1898 consolidation of a multitude of smaller governmental units (Benjamin and Nathan, 2001). The adage of "what is good for the goose is good for the gander" is ignored in the metrocentric state with so much to offer in its rural areas.

Upstate New York experienced its struggles, as post–World War II urbanization, sparked by the massive relocation of people, moved rural residents into the cities from the suburbs. The de-industrialization and disinvestment of the 1970s, spawned by the oil crisis and economic focus on urban blight meant that rural areas, once the "darlings" of federal reformers, were slowly left out of federal and state policies. It did not help the rural upstate area of New York when the political leadership caustically refused assistance to New York City. Albany and the federal government refused a fiscal stabilization package in the 1970s, prompting the New York Times to publish a famous headline: "Ford to City: Drop Dead!"

With the power brokers in State government frequently represented by "Three leaders in a room" negotiations at budget time, the Governor, the Senate Majority Leader, and Speaker of the Assembly have power well and truly focused and centralized. An informal status quo emerged, where the

Speaker of the Assembly hailed from New York City areas, and the Senate Majority leader was "upstate." Governors, elected for two-year terms for most of the State's history, 56 in all from 1777 to the present hailed from around the state. Legislation in New York, as well as budget bills, frequently see "upstate/downstate" provisions, with one example enacted to balance the desires of rent stabilization in the city and a limit on property tax for upstate/ suburbia.

The state has seen an ever-growing secession movement that has only heightened after the 2016 election which seeks to split upstate from downstate. The secessionists feel that the "nanny state" represented by increased gun control legislation limiting ammunition clip sizes impacts and infringes on the hunting culture of rural New York. The "New York Safe Act" is one example of significant identity-based political issues which have divided New York's residents. With upstate cultural identity, tourism, and frankly food security tied to hunting, residents felt that gun control was a "city issue" and the state should refrain from penalizing law-abiding upstate residents with this new rule. As part of the SAFE act, gun shows, often a large fundraiser, and social outlet for collectors and enthusiasts faced steeper regulations, with the laws requiring background checks and waiting periods, and increased fees for licensing and reporting. Many upstate residents felt the SAFE act was an attack on their freedoms, but an undue burden on a hobby and social outlet, and for some organizations, a significant fundraiser in a time when community groups were stretched thin by the loss of local businesses who previously supported philanthropic activities locally.

A second major debate, over the status of hydrofracking created a significant rift in the state. The southern tier, rural and closely aligned to Pennsylvania and Appalachian folkways, wanted to frack for hydrocarbon resources. The city, dependent on water reservoirs in the area, lobbied for pristine preservation. The debate morphed into economics versus environmentalism, and when Governor Cuomo banned fracking, many southern tier residents felt that the city's position had unfairly condemned the area to continued decline. Since communities in the southern tier had pioneered oil prospecting, and had benefited from the prosperity, the residents questioned the logic of honoring the heritage and history but denying the present economic reality and need. Identity politics only serves as a divisive strategy to hide the reality that both the urban and rural areas are intertwined. In examining the coverage of New York's southern tier, classified as part of the Appalachian Regional Commission, I found that the counties are not considered part of Appalachia by researchers engaged in Appalachian studies. Nor do New York residents identify themselves as Appalachian (Jakubowski, forthcoming; Rock and Tabor, 2020).

Another division within the state which influences the "rural deficit narrative" is the regional difference of the state. While New York City is clearly a "New England City" and the Hudson Valley looks east for its affinities, the rest of the state are more "Appalachian" or "Mid-Western" or "Canadian" in their views. With our own perceptions about each other, and the narratives which continue to exaggerate the claims the capital favors down over upstate, our civic and educational worlds are in danger. In my dissertation (Jakubowski, 2019), I saw this divisive narrative repeated online in anonymous chat spaces. The reality is also tangible along the Route 20 and Route 7 corridors, where pro-Trump, anti-Biden, and Confederate flags fly in open spaces. In a recent drive along Route 7, I counted over 50 of those flags in a 70-mile area.

People in upstate's rural areas were angry at what they felt was the arrogance of the reformers from "the city" and "Albany" demanding that their schools get better. Residents, often egged on by politicians in speeches, interviews, and by the local media in op-ed pieces, wanted to know why their communities were "sacrificed" to finance the wealthy downstate. People asserted in these posts the reason was the rural lifestyle. Rural residents in New York, just like the Wisconsin residents from Cramer (2016) resented the urban areas for looking down on rural areas. True seething anger existed in the narrative which posited that their children were attending schools without extracurricular, all so that a downstate student could have a third foreign language.

With the events of January 6, 2021, and the continued unrest among many rural residents towards government at the federal and state levels, our schools have become a battle ground. As resources diminish due to COVID-19, and critical infrastructure needs are held up among partisan battles at the federal and state levels, teachers are burning out and quitting at an alarming rate. Unfortunately, the truth is rural educators in metro dominated states like New York have been leaving rural schools in droves for a long time (Miller, 2012). Recruiting and retaining teachers in rural areas has been an ongoing (dare I say) 100-year-old problem (Biddle and Azano, 2016). Conflict between rural residents and the capital has an equally long history (Justice, 2012). In what were religiously dominated conflicts between different secular camps throughout rural New York, our conflict has now shifted away from religion to ideology.

The research by new voices (Chamberlin, 2020; Miller, 2021; Parton, 2023) have all demonstrated that the rural deficit model does not honor the impactful work that rural communities are undertaking to promote education and engage communities in efforts to include different voices and resources. The work clearly demonstrates that rural regions need support, and we must end the urban normative and metrocentric narratives that other "rural"

Americans. Fulkerson and Thomas (2019) are not wrong in their emphasis on how city-based reformers have gotten rural wrong. It is truly heartening to know that Chamberlin (2020); Miller (2021); and Parton (2023) have created works which emphasize the good in the hollows and hills!

We must change the narrative as educators, policy makers, and scholars. As a profession, we must ensure that OUR narrative reaches the people, the press, and most importantly the politicians. As an educator, you, personally, and your entire circle of professionals and friends must work on a counter narrative by doing public scholarship and interaction. Engage in what Stein and Daniels (2017) called "Going Public." Offer to talk to parents and community members. Write a blog post. Visit other schools to show support. Most importantly, spread on social media the good, the positive, and the profound about your rural education work! Just like the professional athletes have formed their own media outlets, we have podcasts, platforms, and personal narratives which are powerful and offer profound insight. It's time to change the narrative, one teacher at a time.

First, we must start with our education programs. People do not understand how to engage in their local government and civic process. In New York State, we teach civics, and history (as well as geography and economics) from grades K-12, yet for some reason, people do not seem to retain the material. With the publication of nationally revised social studies standards or College, Career, and Civic Life, and changes in the Regents exams, hopefully students and maybe by extension, their parents will understand what civic engagement is (Mantas-Kourounis, 2021).

Second, we must ensure that teachers are truly prepared to teach in rural America. In my current position in a rurally situated teacher preparation program in Upstate New York, many students are from the downstate metro. The students in my classes in fall 2021 semester (of which there were four sections, totaling around 70) contained almost 80 percent who claimed origins from the two counties of Long Island, the five New York City boroughs, Westchester, Rockland, Orange, Putnam, and Dutchess Counties. The students were, because of COVID-19, introduced into local classrooms for the first time. Virtual schooling, since their first year in college, had significantly reduced their ability to engage with local students in the region, of which 100 percent are classified as rural (Jakubowski, 2021).

Third, we must hold politicians accountable for using events and actions for selfish reasons. As many researchers cited above have expressed, schooling fails when individual needs are promoted over community improvement (Cervone, 2017). The continued political narrative of public education as wasteful spending has damaged the ability of educators to have reasonable debates with their communities. While this is not new, as images of teacher union bullying exist in the New York State Archives from the 1970s during a Little Valley Central School District centralization attempt, the rhetoric has escalated to levels which McHenry-Sorber and Schafft (2015) described as disconcerting. Without accountability, then our civil society will disintegrate, starting with our schools. Now with the furor over COVID-19 mask mandates, and the immensely disruptive conflicts over Critical Race Theory, schools are in danger, and rural communities are most in jeopardy (Rhodes et al., 2022).

So is New York State unique? In some ways yes. In comparison to many other urbannormative states (Fulkerson and Thomas, 2019) we are not. We can be a role model and implement best practices to create a positive and supportive environment. Other states may look to New York for examples on citizen research, and community engagement (Jakubowski, forthcoming). Other states' policies, however, should think closely about why the deficit narrative is so persistent, and how to change that stream in engagement. Once New York had a strong tradition of research and practice on rural education. It is time to re-energize that tradition, and ensure practices and research see publication and implementation.

Conclusion

What Should We Do from Here?

This book was, and is a highly personal journey (Ellis et al., 2011), which required extensive revisions following the COVID-19 pandemic. My own personal journey in rural America, and specifically New York State, led me to ask what I thought was a reasonable question: Why do so many rural school consolidations in New York fail? How naive I was! Researching rural education is a journey into the dusty past, and present conflagration. The future is a non-Newtonian fluid, like Jell-O (invented in rural New York's Leroy Village). I learned, as a suburban child, how much I did not know about rural areas. Attending college at SUNY Fredonia and competing field experiences in the small schools surrounding the area, I had no idea what my professional journey would entail (Jakubowski, 2021).

As a teacher, first in rural Western New York's southern tier, and then in Central Southern Tier New York, and living and working in two of the more rural counties in the state, I saw a marked difference, in my opinion, between what happened in our schools in New York State. Yet my students, in rural communities, were expected to perform just as well on the Regent's exams, as I was, from one of the top-performing suburban districts in the number two metro area in the state.

So, how to organize the research questions? Essentially, how do I examine what was, is, and could be in rural research? As a trained historian, I wanted to examine the history or rural school consolidation in the state. I sought and discovered records in the New York State Archives and the resources from the Reorganization Files. In the age before the internet really matured (2000–2004), finding information, accessing source materials, and writing the history of communities engaged in consolidation was just beyond my reach. I am not going to lie, I really could have tried harder, but my calling at that moment was teaching secondary social studies education.

After leaving active teaching, and moving on to the State Education Department, and starting a different route, that of policy analysis, and thankfully the maturing internet, I began to find that my research question was quite old. People who had worked in the building I worked in had wrestled with what to do about New York's rural schools. I discovered in my professional day work, the State was still using the 1958 Master Plan, and I wondered why. I also became aware of the amount of online discussion about school consolidation, and how people felt freed to write whatever they felt was the truth online, away from the gaze, and judgment of people within, and just beyond the community. So, I decided to look at what people said online, and I found, through the dissertation and class process, Kingdon (2011) and Scott (1990). In finding the two scholars, I also found a community of educators who had come before me at the master granting institutions and doctoral research centers across the state. My predecessors had wrangled with the very question of rural schools. Their research, in the physical spaces, and electronic databases, are practically unmined. A future project of specifically examining those theses and dissertations awaits the keyboard!

WHAT DID THIS BOOK DO?

Any book written should have a purpose. This one created an exploratory study through some exemplary case study (Stake, 1995) examples of rural schools in what Fulkerson and Thomas (2019) call an urban normative state. Centered on autoethnography, I tried to reflect on my own personal experience, and what others experienced through similar events (Ellis et al., 2011). The book specifically examined how a one-hundred-year-old policy of promoting rural school consolidation in New York was reaffirmed multiple times, even amid voter disagreement. New York's policymakers, based in Albany, New York, with quite a few from downstate, continue to promote consolidation as a solution to improving efficiency and effectiveness in rural schools. The book also examined, in chapter 1, how Kingdon's (2011) problem, policy, and politics streams can help us understand how the rural school consolidation efforts re-emerge in each community. The chapter identified how communities, their leadership, and policy makers can decide that, yes, a problem exists within the school, and something must be done. In the process of identifying the three streams which Kingdon (2011) proposed, I found that the politics stream is often the failure, as communities will vote with their emotions, because they do not trust consolidation is the only solution which is viable.

A specific case study presented in chapter 2 examined what people said about consolidation on an online discussion platform. The results indicated that most attacks were personal in nature. There are posts that were substantive and were in alignment with national research on rural consolidation, except that identity was not the overwhelming factor for the defeat. Rather, the sources from the consolidation attempt revealed questions about economic efficiency, programmatic enhancement, and a potential state mandate to consolidate.

In chapter 3, I examined a failed consolidation using the Kingdon (2011) multiple streams model. The exemplar case study (Stake, 1995) found using materials from the online discussions website Topix residents within the communities engaged in consolidation reporting a different narrative from what school officials and the media reported about the advantages of the process and results. I found that people reported that voters would defeat the consolidation due to a tax rate still too high, even after the application of state aid. Other alternatives to consolidation were available, and the online discussion indicated that consolidation should be a last resort. Third, posts identified a lack of trust in the messaging local school leaders provided to community members concerning the proposed merger. The lack of trust in school officials from within this community is disturbing, as it is part of a larger distrust in elected and appointed government officials.

In chapter 4, I compare New York State government policy on rural and urban education. I explore how the State has, over the past almost 100 years, called for consolidation, despite the lack of evidence in support of this policy. I also examine how state policymakers have privileged urban areas in the implementation of policy and financial decisions. I explain how this urban normative policy implementation has created anger within rural residents, who wonder who represents their interests.

Chapter 5 examines the state of rural schools in New York and asks if school consolidation is even the answer to helping rural areas with educational opportunities. I also examine the concept of a Wicked Problem. While most rural schools face significant infrastructure issues, due to policies which have disadvantaged those areas in the past, the Wicked Problem theory clearly states no easy answer is forthcoming. New York's bureaucrats however, need to rethink their insistence on consolidation as the silver bullet, especially with opposition to the policy. The 1958 Master Plan and the continued political rhetoric which is focusing on the finances of schools misses a solid rationale: ALL students in New York State deserve a world class education.

A case study presented in chapter 6 shows how communities who lose their schools are dramatically impacted. With the loss of the schools, these areas experienced first a sense of betrayal, as studies often promise the continuation of at least elementary programming in one or more of the communities. The economic, social, and political implications of building closures just add fuel to the debate that school consolidation is inappropriate for most communities.

Chapter 7 dives deeply into the state of New York, and if it is unique, or just one of fifty states. I argue that the history and traditions of the state are unique, but not exceptional. Rather, the state should return to its roots as a leading researcher and practitioner center for rural education in the United States. I also stress the need to reinvigorate the traditions of sharing our experiences with other states, and hopefully answer Their et al.'s (2021) call for research in the underrepresented Northeast region.

As our technology, pedagogy, policy, practice, and professional development advance, we should see changes in opportunities for our rural areas. What is most critical, though, is the end of the deficit narrative which is overwhelmingly reported in media and research. Fortunately, with the efforts of multiple rural facing groups, and research communities, we are slowly changing the research narrative. Our next assignment is changing the minds of the media and policy maker's minds. These goals may only happen if, and when, significant local voices emerge, and priorities change from a deficit narrative to a rural centric form of social justice.

References

Abshier, W. et al. (2011). "Superintendent Perspectives of Financial Survival Strategies in Small School Districts." *Rural Educator* 32(3), 1–10.

Adams, Jr., J. and E.M. Foster. (2002). "District Size and State Educational Costs: Should Consolidation Follow School Finance Reform?" *Journal of Education Finance* 27(3), 833–855.

Ajayi, L. (2014). "Innovative and Effective Teaching Methods for Place-Based Teacher Preparation in Rural Communities." *Education Research for Policy and Practice* 13(3), 251–268.

Alexander, K. & M. Alexander. (2011). *American Public School Law*, 8th ed. Independence, KY: Wadsworth Publishing.

Al-Muslim, A. (2013). "Hempstead Board Votes to Scrap Academy System." *Newsday* downloaded from: http://www.newsday.com/long-island/towns/hempstead-school-board-votes-to-scrap-academy-system-1.5143057

Alsbury, T. (2008). "School Board Member and Superintendent Turnover and Influence on Student Achievement: An Application of the Dissatisfaction Theory." *Leadership and Policy in Schools* 7: 202–229.

Alsbury, T. and Shaw, N. (2005). "Policy implications for Social Justice in School District Consolidation." *Leadership and Policy in Schools* 4: 105–126.

Ananthakrishnan, V. (2005). "The Challenge of Defining Equity and Adequacy in State School Finance Systems: A Look at New York's Experience." *Policy Perspectives* 19–29.

Andrews, J.A. (2014). *An Exploration of Factors Leading to Shared Superintendencies in New York State* (Doctoral dissertation, Sage Graduate School).

Anrig, G. R. (1963). "Sociological Factors Which Resist School Consolidations." *The Clearing House: A Journal of Educational Strategies, Issues and Ideas* 38(3), 161–164.

Anthony-Stevens, V., & Langford, S. (2020). "'What Do You Need a Course Like That For?' Conceptualizing Diverse Ruralities in Rural Teacher Education." *Journal of Teacher Education* 71(3), 332–344.

Appalachian Regional Commission (2022). Classifying Economic Distress in Appalachia.

References

Arnold, M., et al. (2005). "A Look at the Condition of Rural Education Research." *Journal of Research in Rural Education* 20.6.

Associated Press. (2012). "Cornell Study: Population of Adirondacks Hamilton County ontinues to Decline." Downloaded from: http://www.syracuse.com/news/index.ssf/2012/04/new_york_study_population_of_a.html

Avery, L. M., & Hains, B. J. (2017). "Oral Traditions: A Contextual Framework for Complex Science Concepts—Laying the Foundation for a Paradigm of Promise in Rural Science Education." *Cultural Studies of Science Education* 12(1), 129–166.

Azano, A.P., et al., (2020). *Teaching in Rural Places.* New York: Routledge.

Azano, A. P., Eppley, K., & Biddle, C. (Eds.). (2021). *The Bloomsbury Handbook of Rural Education in the United States*. New York: Bloomsbury Publishing.

Azano, A. P., & Stewart, T. T. (2015). "Exploring Place and Practicing Justice: Preparing Pre-service Teachers for Success in Rural Schools." *Journal of Research in Rural Education (Online)* 30(9), 1.

Bader, D. (2012). "After Merger Failure Valley Districts Consider their Options." Utica Observer Dispatch. Available from: http://www.uticaod.com/news/x1292878762/After-merger-failure-Valley-districts-consider-their-options

Bard, J. et al. (2006). "Rural School Consolidation: History, Research Summary, Conclusions, and Recommendations." *The Rural Educator* 27(2), 40–48.

Barley, Z. and N. Brigham. (2008). *Preparing Teachers to Teach in Rural Schools.* Washington, DC: IES RELC. Available at: ies.ed.gov/ncee/edlabs.

Barrett, N., Cowen, J., Toma, E., & Troske, S. (2015). "Working with What They Have: Professional Development as a Reform Strategy in Rural Schools." *Journal of Research in Rural Education (Online)* 30(10), 1.

Baumgartner, F. (2016). "John Kingdon and the Evolutionary Approach to Public Policy and Agenda Setting," in N. Zahariadis, ed. *Handbook of Public Policy Agenda Setting.* Cheltenham, UK: Edward Elgar Publishing.

Baumgartner, F. & B. Jones. (1993). *Agendas and Instability in American Politics.* Chicago, IL: University of Chicago Press.

Beadie, N. (2008). Tuition Funding for Common Schools. *Social Science History* 32(1), 107–133.

Beigh, M. (2018). The 1837 Westfield Academy. Downloaded: https://westfieldny.com/living-here/1837-westfield-academy-described-elderly-resident-over-ninety-years-ago

Benjamin, G. and R. Nathan. (2001). *Regionalism and Realism.* Washington, DC: Brookings Institute.

Berger, M. L. (1972). Community Control of Schools: The Rural Precedent. *Contemporary Education* 43(6), 309.

Berkman, M. B. (2005). *Ten Thousand Democracies: Politics and Public Opinion in America's School Districts*. Washington, DC: Georgetown University Press.

Bernsen, N. R., Crandall, M. S., Leahy, J. E., & Biddle, C. (2022). How Far to Go? Community Influences on Youth Educational Aspirations in Rural, Resource-Dependent Places. *RSF: The Russell Sage Foundation Journal of the Social Sciences*, 8(3), 189–207.

Berry, C. and M. West. (2008). "Growing Pains: The school Consolidation Movement and Student Outcomes." *Journal of Law, Economics and Organization* 26.1, 1–29.

Berry, C. (2006/7). "School Consolidation and Inequality." *Brookings Papers on Educational Policy* 9, 49–75.

Berry, F. & W. Berry. (1990). "State Lottery Adoptions as Policy Innovations." *The American Political Science Review* Vol. 84, No. 2., 395–415.

Biddle, C., & Azano, A. P. (2016). "Constructing and Reconstructing the 'Rural School Problem': A Century of Rural Education Research." *Review of Research in Education* 40(1), 298–325.

Biddle, C., Sutherland, D. H., & McHenry-Sorber, E. (2019). "On Resisting 'Awayness' and Being a Good Insider: Early Career Scholars Revisit Coladarci's Swan Song a Decade Later. *Journal of Research in Rural Education (Online)* 35(7), 1–16.

Birkland, T. (2001). *An Introduction to the Policy Process*. Amonk, NY: ME Sharpe.

Blauwkamp, J. et al. (2011). "School Consolidation in Nebraska: Economic Efficiency vs. Rural Community Life." *Online Journal of Rural Research and Policy* 6(1), 1–20.

Bohrson, R. G. (1962). Bibliography, Rural Education and the Small School. Eric reproduction services.

Brasington, D. (1999). "The Joint Provision of Public Goods. *Journal of Public Economics* 73.3, (373–393).

Brasington, D. (2003). "Snobbery, Racism or Mutual Distaste?" *Review of Economics and Statistics* 85.4, 874–883.

Brenner, D., Presley, B., Conradi, J., Rodolfich, W., & Hansford, T. (2020). "Get Connected Now: A Conversation with School Leaders and Policy Makers about Expanding Rural Broadband Access." *The Rural Educator* 41(3), 57–62.

Brent, B. O., Sipple, J. W., Killeen, K. M., & Wischnowski, M. W. (2004). "Stalking Cost-Effective Practices in Rural Schools." *Journal of Education Finance* 29(3), 237–256.

Brown, D. & Schafft, K. (2011). *Rural People and Communities in the 21st Century: Resilience and Transformation*. New York: Polity.

Butler, A., & Sinclair, K. A. (2020). "Place Matters: A Critical Review of Place Inquiry and Spatial Methods in Education Research." *Review of Research in Education* 44(1), 64–96.

Cairney, P. & M. Jones. (2015). "Kingdon's Multiple Streams Approach: What is the Empirical Impact of this Universal Theory?" *The Policy Studies Journal.* Published online preview article. Volume and Issue numbers forthcoming as of November 10, 2015.

Campbell-Halfaker, D. C., & Gregor, M. A. (2021). The Importance of Cultural Context in Rural Education: Historical and Modern Perspectives. *Psychology from the Margins* 3(1), 3.

Canales, M. et al. (2010). "Superintendents/Principals in Small Rural School Districts: A Qualitative Study of Dual Roles." *International Journal of Educational Leadership Preparation* 5(1).

Canter, G. (1986). School District Reorganization: A Qualified Success. Ithaca, NY: State University of New York. (ERIC Document services).

Carr, P. & M. Kefalas. (2009). *Hollowing Out the Middle: The Rural Brain Drain and What it Means for America.* Boston, MA: Beacon Press.

Casto, H. (2012). "Potential Synergy: Rural School Districts and International Student Programs." *Rural Educator* 34.1, 1–11.

Casto, H. G. (2016). "Just One More Thing I Have to Do": School-Community Partnerships. *School Community Journal* 26(1), 139–162.

Casto, H. G. (2019). "'We're Nine Miles from the Board Building, but the Perception is that We're 100 Miles Away out in Farm Country': The Case of a Rural School in a Non-rural District." *Journal of Rural Studies* 72, 164–173.

Casto, H., McGrath, B., Sipple, J. W., & Todd, L. (2016). "Community Aware" Education Policy: Enhancing Individual and Community Vitality. *Education Policy Analysis Archives/Archivos Analíticos de Políticas Educativas* 24, 1–30.

Catte, E. (2018). *What You Are Getting Wrong about Appalachia.* Cleveland, OH: Belt Publishing.

Cervone, J. A. (2017). *Corporatizing Rural Education: Neoliberal Globalization and Reaction in the United States.* New York: Springer.

Chabe, L. (2011). Putting the Pieces Together: A Research Based Handbook for School District Administrators and Board of Education Members that Examines School Consolidation and the Process of a Merger Feasibility Study. Unpublished PhD Diss. State University of New York at Buffalo.

Chalker, D. (1999). "Politics and Decision Making: The Rural Scene," in Chalker, ed. *Leadership for Rural Schools*: *Lessons for all Educators.* Lancaster, PA: Technomic Publishing Co., Inc., pp. 25–62.

Chamberlin, R. (2020). Stronger with Each Other. Unpublished PhD Diss. University of Minnesota.

Chambers, C., Crumb, L., & Harris, C. (2019). "A Call for Dreamkeepers in Rural United States: Considering the Postsecondary Aspirations of Rural Ninth Graders." *Theory & Practice in Rural Education* 9(1), 7–22.

Chiles, R. (2018). *The Revolution of '28: Al Smith, American Progressivism, and the Coming of the New Deal.* Ithaca, NY: Cornell University Press.

Churchill, C. (2023). "What about Up State's Population Decline?" *Albany Times Union.* https://www.timesunion.com/churchill/article/Churchill-But-what-about-upstate-s-population-17725039.php

Clark, B. (1972). "The Organizational Saga in Higher Education." *Administrative Science Quarterly* 17: 178–184.

Clark, J. B., Leslie, W. B., & O'Brien, K. P. (Eds.). (2010). *SUNY at Sixty: The Promise of the State University of New York.* Albany, NY: SUNY Press.

Clark, S. (2014). "Envisioning Schoolhouse Nostalgia and the Pastoral Retreat: A Rural Landscape Approach to Educational History." *American Educational History Journal* 41(1/2), 255.

Cobb, R. & C. Elder. (1983). *Participation in American Politics,* 2nd ed. Baltimore, MD: The Johns Hopkins University Press.

Corbett, M. (2007). *Learning to Leave: The Irony of Schooling in a Coastal Community*. Halifax, NS: Fernwood Publishing.

Corbett, M. (2015). "Towards a Rural Sociological Imagination." *Ethnography and Education* 10.3, 263–277.

Corbett, M. (2005). "Rural Education and Out-Migration." *Canadian Journal of Education* 28(1/2), 52–72.

Corbett, M. (2009). "No Time to Fool Around with the Wrong Education." *Rural Society* 19(2). 163–177.

Corbett, M. (2014). "The Ambivalence of Community: A Critical Analysis of Rural Education's Oldest Trope." *Peabody Journal of Education* 89(5), 603–618.

Corbett, M., & Gereluk, D. (Eds.). (2020). *Rural Teacher Education: Connecting Land and People*. Singapore: Springer Nature.

Corbett, M. (2021). "Re-placing Rural Education: AERA Special Interest Group on Rural Education Career Achievement Award Lecture." *Journal of Research in Rural Education* (Online) 37(3), 1–14.

Corbett, M., & Tinkham, J. (2014). "Small Schools in a Big World: Thinking about a Wicked Problem." *Alberta Journal of Educational Research* 60(4), 691–707.

Cordova, R. A., & Reynolds, W. M. (2020). *Educating for Social Justice: Field Notes from Rural Communities*. Boston: Brill.

Cornell, S. (1999). *The Other Founders*. Chapel Hill, NC: UNC Press.

Craig, S. (2016). "New York's Southern Tier, Once a Home for Big Business, Is Struggling." *New York Times*. Downloaded: nytimes.com/2015/09/03.

Cramer, K. J. (2016). *The Politics of Resentment: Rural Consciousness in Wisconsin and the Rise of Scott Walker*. Chicago, IL: University of Chicago Press.

Cross, A. (2018). "'Stop Overlooking Us!': Missed Intersections of Trump, Media, and Rural America." In *The Trump Presidency, Journalism, and Democracy*. Oxford: Routledge, 231–256.

Cubberly, E. (1914). *Rural Life and Education*. Boston, MA: Houghton Mifflin.

Davidson, O. (1996). *Broken Heartland: The Rise of America's Rural Ghetto*. Iowa City: University of Iowa Press.

Dawson, J. (2015). Remarks at the CARDI Annual Conference. Downloaded: https://cardi.cals.cornell.edu/programs/rsa/activities/conference

Deal, T. & K. Peterson. (1999). *Shaping School Culture*. San Francisco, CA: Jossey Bass.

Deantoni, E. (1971). "Coming of Age in the Industrial State: The Ideology of Implementation of Rural School Reform 1893–1925." PhD Diss, Cornell University.

Dearing, J. & E. Rogers. (1996). *Agenda Setting*. Thousand Oaks, CA: Sage.

Deitz, R. (2005). "The Regional Economy of Upstate New York." *Federal Reserve Branch of Buffalo*. Available from: http://www.newyorkfed.org/research/regional_economy/upstate/winter05.pdf

DeYoung, A. (1991). *Struggling With Their Histories: Economic Decline and Educational Improvement in Four Rural Southeastern School Districts*. Norwood, NJ: Ablex Publishing.

DeYoung A. (1995). *The Life and Death of a Rural American High School.* New York: Garland.

DeYoung, A. and C. Howley. (1990). "The Political Economy of Rural School Consolidation." *Peabody Journal of Education* 67.4, 63–89.

Dhaliwal, T. K., & Bruno, P. (2021). The Rural/Nonrural Divide? K–12 District Spending and Implications of Equity-based School Funding. *AERA Open* 7, 2332858420982549.

Dinki, T. (2018). "New York State School Districts Resist Mergers." *Olean Times Herald.* From The State of New York Rural Schools: Left Behind Series. https://www.oleantimesherald.com/news/new-york-state-school-districts-communities-and-even-government-resist/article_eae4fb7a-da4a-11e8-8342-c76b1f4898cb.html

Doukas, D. (2003). *Worked Over.* Ithaca, NY: Cornell University Press.

Duncan, C. (1999). *Worlds Apart: Why Poverty Persists in Rural America.* New Haven, CT: Yale University Press.

Duncombe, W. and J. Yinger. (2007). "Does School District Consolidation Cut Costs?" *Education Finance and Policy* 2.7, 341–375.

Dunkirk Observer. (2013). "Goodell will Continue the Push for Regional High Schools." *Dunkirk Observer* Online. Downloaded: https://www.observertoday.com/news/page-one/2013/04/goodell-will-continue-push-for-regional-high-schools/

Dupéré, V., Goulet, M., Archambault, I., Dion, E., Leventhal, T., & Crosnoe, R. (2019). "Circumstances Preceding Dropout Among Rural High School Students: A Comparison with Urban Peers." *Journal of Research in Rural Education* 35(3).

Dzikowski, D. (2012). Testimony to the New New York Education Reform Commission. Available: http://www.governor.ny.gov/sites/governor.ny.gov/files/archive/assets/documents/102212_fingerlakeshearing/DeniseDzikowskiTestimony.pdf\

Easton, B. (2012). "Albany's Unkindest Cut of All." *New York Times.* Available at: http://www.nytimes.com/2012/05/26/opinion/the-danger-in-school-spending-cuts.html?_r=0

Edwards, D. S. (2021). "Over the River and through the Woods: The Role of Distance in Participation in Rural School Choice." *Journal of School Choice* 1–31.

Eissler, R., et al. (2014). "New Avenues for the Study of Agenda Setting." *Policy Studies Journal* 42.s1, S71–S86.

Ellis, C., Adams, T. E., & Bochner, A. P. (2011). "Autoethnography: An Overview." *Historical Social Research/Historische sozialforschung* Vol. 36, No. 4, 273–290.

Enberg, J., et al. (2011). Closing Schools in a Shrinking District. Paper downloaded from: https://www.sree.org/conferences/2011/program/downloads/abstracts/34.pdf

Eppley, K. (2015). "'Hey, I Saw Your Grandparents at Walmart': Teacher Education for Rural Schools and Communities." *The Teacher Educator*, 50(1), 67–86.

Essert, P. and R. Howard. (1952). *Education Planning by neighborhoods in Centralized Districts.* New York: Teachers College Press.

Evans, R. (1996). *The Human Side of School Change: Reform, Resistance, and the Real-Life Problems of Innovation. The Jossey-Bass Education Series.* San Francisco, CA: Jossey-Bass, Inc.

Ewing, E. and T. Green (2022). Beyond the Headlines. *Educational Research*, 51(1), 58–65.

Fairman, J. & C. Donis-Keller. (2012). "School District Reorganization in Maine." *Maine Policy Review* 21.2, 24–40.

Farley, A. N., Childs, J., & Johnson, O. (2019). "Preparing Leaders for Wicked Problems? How the Revised PSEL and NELP Standards Address Equity and Justice." *Education Policy Analysis Archives* 27, 115–115.

Farrie, D., & Sciarra, D. G. (2022). "Making the Grade 2021: How Fair Is School Funding in Your State?" *Education Law Center*.

Farmer, T. et al., (2006). "Adequate Yearly Progress in Small Rural Schools and Rural Low Income Schools." *The Rural Educator* 27(3).

Feldmann, D. (2003). *Curriculum and the American Rural School.* University Press of America.

Ferris, J. (October 19, 2012). "Official: With merger voted down, taxes will go up or massive school cuts will be made." Downloaded from http://www.wktv.com/news/local/Official-With-school-merger-voted-down-taxes-will-go-up-or-there-will-be-massive-school-cuts-175011491.html

Fischel, W. A. (2005). "The Homevoter Hypothesis." Cambridge, MA: Harvard University Press.

Fischel, W. (2010). "Nether Creatures of State of Accidents of Geography." *University of Chicago Law Review* 77, 177–199.

Fitchen, J. (1991). *Endangered Spaces, Enduring Places: Change, Identity, and Survival in Rural America.* Boulder, CO: Westview Press.

Flora, C., J. Flora, & S. Gasteyer. (2016). *Rural Communities: Legacy and Challenges,* 5th ed. Boulder, CO: Westview Press.

Folts, J. D. (1996). *History of the University of the State of New York and the State Education Department 1784–1996.* Albany, NY: NYSED.

Foster, J. (2015). School Consolidation and Community Cohesion in One Rural Kansas Community. Unpublished Master's Thesis. Kansas State University, Manhattan, KS.

Fulkerson, G. & A. Thomas. (2016). *Reinventing Rural: New Realities in an Urbanizing World.* Lexington Press.

Fulkerson, G. M. & Thomas, A. R. (2019). *Urbanormativity: Reality, Representation, and Everyday Life*. Lanham, MD: Rowman & Littlefield.

Fuller, W. (1982). *The Old Country School.* Chicago, IL: University of Chicago Press.

Gallo, J. (2020). "Against the Grain: Narratives of Rural Teachers' Professional Lives." *Rural Educator* 41(2), 1–13.

Galvin, P. (2000). "Organizational Boundaries, Authority, and School District Organization." In Theobald and Malen, eds. *Balancing Local Control and State Responsibility for K-12 Education.* Larchmont, NY: Eye on Education.

Galway, et al. (2013). The Impact Centralization On Local School District Governance in Canada. *Canadian Journal of Educational Administration and Policy* 145.

Gamson, D. A., & Hodge, E. M. (2016). "Education Research and the Shifting Landscape of the American School District, 1816 to 2016." *Review of Research in Education*, 40(1), 216–249.

Gee, J. P. (2014). *Unified Discourse Analysis: Language, Reality, Virtual Worlds, and Video Games*. Oxford: Routledge.

Gettleman, M. E. (1969). "Romance and Educational Policy: John H. Finley's Inspirational Efforts as New York State Commissioner of Education, 1913–1920." *Paedagogica Historica* 9(1–2), 380–399.

Gioia, D. & J. Thomas. (1996). "Identity Image and Issue Interpretation: Sensemaking during Strategic Change in Academia." *Administrative Science Quarterly* 41: 370–403.

Glassberg, D. (2001). *Sense of History: The Place of the Past in American Life*. Amherst, MA: University of Massachusetts Press.

Goodlad, J. I. (2004). *Romances with Schools: A Life of Education*. New York: McGraw Hill Professional.

Gordon, M. (2015). A Study of the Impact of School Consolidation on Student Advancement and District Financial Health. Unpublished EdD Diss. University of St. Francis, Joliet, IL.

Gordon, N. and B. Knight. (2008). "The Effects of School District Consolidation on Educational Cost and Quality." *Public Finance Review* 36, 408–430.

Gordon, N. and B. Knight. (2009). "A Spatial Estimator with an Application to School District Consolidation." *Journal of Public Economics* 92, 752–765.

Gordon, J. and J. Patterson. (2008). "It's What We've Always Been Doing." *Journal of Educational Change* 9, 17–35.

Gormley, M. (2013). "Cuomo to Strapped NY Cities, Schools: Merge." Retrieved from: http://news.yahoo.com/cuomo-strapped-ny-cities-schools-182321047.html

Grant, J. (2013). North Country Schools Face Uncharted Territory. Downloaded: http://www.northcountrypublicradio.org/news/story/21779/20130411/north-country-schools-face-uncharted-ground

Greco, J. (2007). *Teacher Migration out of Rural School Districts: An Analysis of Teacher Recruitment and Retention Issues in Three Rural School Districts in New York State*. PhD diss. University at Albany.

Haddad, M. and T. Alsbury. (2008). "Using Spatial Analysis to Examine Student Proficiency." *Planning and Changing* 39.1&2, 98–126.

Haller, E., J. Nusser, D. Monk. (1999). "Assessing School District Quality." In D. Chalker, Ed. *Leadership for Rural Schools*. Lancaster, PA: Technomic Publications.

Haller, E. and D. Monk. (1988). "New Reforms, Old Reforms and the Consolidation of Rural Schools." *Educational Administrative Quarterly* 24.4, 470–483.

Haller, E. J., Monk, D. H., Bear, A. S., Griffith, J., & Moss, P. (1990). "School Size and Program Comprehensiveness: Evidence from High School and Beyond." *Educational Evaluation and Policy Analysis* 12(2), 109–120.

Harbatkin, E. (2022). Staffing for School Turnaround in Rural Settings. *Leadership and Policy in Schools* 1–23.

Harkins, A., & McCarroll, M. (2019). *Appalachian Reckoning: A Region Responds to Hillbilly Elegy*. Morgantown: West Virginia University Press.

Hasnat, M. A., and Greenwood, J. "Schools Celebrating Place and Community." *Australian and International Journal of Rural Education* 31, no. 3 (2021), 81–95.

Hauptman, L. M. (2001). *Conspiracy of Interests: Iroquois dispossession and the Rise of New York State*. Syracuse, NY: Syracuse University Press.

Heffernan, K. M. (2021). "'Much More Chewing': A Case Study of Resistance to School Reform in Rural New York during the Early Twentieth Century." *Paedagogica Historica* 1–19.

Henig, J. "The Politics of Localism in an Era of Centralization, Privatization and Choice." In R.L. Crowson and E.B. Goldrong, eds. *The New Localism in American Education. The 108th Yearbook of the National Society of the Study of Education* 1, 112–129.

Henig, J. (2009). "Mayors, Governors, and Presidents." *Peabody Journal of Education* 84.3, 283–299.

Hess, F. M., & Eden, M. (Eds.). (2021). *The Every Student Succeeds Act (ESSA): What it Means for Schools, Systems, and States*. Cambridge, MA: Harvard Education Press.

Hibbard, M. (2012). A Conversation with: Mike Linehan, president and CEO of the Yates County Chamber of Commerce. Downloaded from: http://www.fltimes.com/news/local/article_213c31d6-00cf-11e2-8e29-0019bb2963f4.html

Highland Press. (2012). http://www.ellicottvilletimes.com/2012/04/20/cattaraugus-little-valley-school-closing-update/

Howlett, M., et al. (2015). "Forum Section: Theoretically Refining the Multiple Streams Framework." *European Journal of Political Research* 54, 419–434.

Howley, C., & Redding, S. (Eds.). (2021). *Cultivating Rural Education: A People-focused Approach for States*. IAP.

Howley, A. et al. (2012). "Stretching to Survive: District Autonomy in an Age of Dwindling Resources." *JRRE 27.3*.

Howley, C. et al. (2011). *Consolidation of Schools and Districts: What the Research Says and What it Means*. Working paper, National Education Policy Center.

Howley A. and C. Howley. (2006). "Small Schools and the Pressure to Consolidate." *Education Policy Analysis Archives* 14.10.

Howley, C. and J. Eckman. (1997). *Sustainable Small Schools*. Charlestown, WV: AEL Clearinghouse.

Howley, C. & C. Howley. (2015.) "Farming the Poor," in K. Sturges, ed. *Neoliberalizing Educational Reform*. Rotterdam: Sense Publishing, 23–51.

Howley, C. and A. Howley. (2010). "Poverty and Achievement in Rural School Communities." In E. K. Schafft and A. Youngblood Jackson, *Rural Education for the Twenty-First Century*. University Park, PA: Pennsylvania State University Press, 34–50.

Jacobs, N. and B. Munis. (2022). Staying in Place: Federalism and the Political Economy. *Publis: The Journal of Federalism*, 50(4): 544–65.

Jakubowski, C. (2004). Masters Level Research Presentation. SUNY Binghamton Department of History Colloquium, spring.

Jakubowski, C. (2013). Unforced Neighbors: Rural School Community and Crises. Paper presented at Institutions and Societies, SUNY Albany Graduate Student Conference.

Jakubowski, C. (2014a). Losing Our Schools, Losing Our Future: A Community's Reaction to a Failed School Consolidation Vote. Paper presented at the University of Rochester Graduate Student Conference.

Jakubowski, C. (2014b). Reform and Identity in Rural New York Schools. Paper presented at Researching New York Conference. http://www.nystatehistory.org/rsny2014-program-10-21pm.pdf

Jakubowski, C. (2014c) Why are We Leaving Rural Students Behind? 7th Annual Conference on Equity and Social Justice. http://7thannualconferenceonequity2014.sched.org/event/63aa374c060595765d5294d6aedb8af9#.VjgBb7erTIU

Jakubowski, C. (2014d). Gilded Paychecks and Benefits Packages: Beyond Identity and State Mandates in Rural School Consolidation. Paper Presented at Institutions and Societies, SUNY Albany Graduate Student Conference.

Jakubowski, C. (2019a). Urban-Normative Reforms Missing the Mark. *Australian and International Journal of Rural Education* 29(3), 92–104.

Jakubowski, C. T. (2019b). *Hidden Resistance in Rural Education: A Study of Two School District Consolidation Attempts in New York State 2008–2014*. State University of New York at Albany.

Jakubowski, C. (2020a). *Thinking About Teaching*. Alexandra, VA: Edumatch Publishing.

Jakubowski, C. (2020b). Rural New York Reforms. Paper presented to the Organization of Education Historians.

Jakubowski, C. (2021). *A Cog in the Machine*. Alexandra, VA: Edumatch Publishing.

Jakubowski, C. (forthcoming). Northern Appalachia, or Rural New York? Submitted to the *Journal of Appalachia Studies*.

James, J., & Wyckoff, J. (2020). Teacher Labor Markets: An Overview. *The Economics of Education*, 355–370.

Jennings, J. (2001). "Title I: Its Legislative History and Promise." In G. Borman, et al., eds. *Title I: Compensatory Education at the Crossroads*. Mahwah, NJ: Lawrence Erlbaum Associates, 1–26.

Jimerson, L. (2005). Placism in NCLB—How Rural Children are Left Behind, *Equity & Excellence in Education,* 38:3, 211–219.

Jimerson, L. (2002). "Inter-District Open Enrollment: The Benign Choice." *The Clearing House* 76.1: 16–19.

Johnson, K. et al. (1995). "Local Government Fiscal Burden in Non-metropolitan America." *Rural Sociology* 60.3, 381–398.

Johnson, J., & Howley, C. B. (2015). Contemporary Federal Education Policy and Rural Schools: A Critical Policy Analysis. *Peabody Journal of Education*, 90(2), 224–241.

Johnson, A., Kuhfeld, M., & Soland, J. (2021). The Forgotten 20%: Achievement and Growth in Rural Schools Across the Nation. *AERA Open*, 7, 23328584211052046.

Johnson, O. (2014). Still Separate, Still Unequal. *The Journal of Negro Education*, 83(3), 199–215.

Joinson, A. (1999). "Social Desirability, Anonymity, and Internet Based Questionnaires." *Behavior Research, Methods and Computers* 31.3, 433–438.

Jones, M., et al. (2015). "A River Runs Through It: A Multiple Streams Meta Review." *The Policy Studies Journal.* Online preview, volume and issue to be determined, November 10, 2015.

Jordan, L., Kostandini, G., & Mykerezi, E. (2012). Rural and Urban High School Dropout Rates: Are They Different? *Journal of Research in Rural Education* (Online), 27(12), 1.

Justice, B. (2004). "Bones of Contention." *New York History* 85.2, 123–148.

Justice, B. (2012). *War That Wasn't: Religious Conflict and Compromise in the Common Schools of New York State, 1865–1900.* Albany, NY: SUNY Press.

Kachris, P. T. (1987). *A History of the District Superintendency and BOCES, 1910–1982* (Doctoral dissertation, Syracuse University).

Kaestle, C. (1983). *Pillars of The Republic.* New York: Hill and Wang.

Kaestle, C. & A. Lodewick, eds. (2007). *To Educate a Nation: Federal and National Strategies of School Reform.* Lawrence, KS: University of Kansas Press.

Kamenetz, A. (2021). A Look at the Groups Supporting School Board Protests Nationwide. *NPR.* Downloaded: https://www.npr.org/2021/10/26/1049078199/a-look-at-the-groups-supporting-school-board-protesters-nationwide

Kamrath, B. (2022). Revisiting the Revolving Door of Rural Superintendent Turnover. *The Rural Educator,* 43(2), 16–33.

Katz, M. B. (1987). *Reconstructing American Education.* Harvard University Press.

Kaushal, N. et al., (2011). How is Family Income Related to Investments in Children's Learning? In Duncan and Murnane, eds. *Whither Opportunity?: Rising Inequality, Schools and Children's Life Chances.* New York: Russell Sage Foundation, 187–206.

Kearns, B. (1992). *An Analysis of State Education Mandates as Interpreted by Superintendents of Rural K-12 Districts in New York.* PhD Diss. Albany, NY: SUNY.

Kelly, A. (2007). "Resistance to School Consolidation in Rural Appalachian Community." Master's Thesis: VPI.

Killeen, K. M., & Sipple, J. W. (2006). *Upstate School Reform: The Challenge of Regional Geography.* Metropolitan Policy Program, Brookings Institution.

King, Jr., J. (2012). Presentation to NYSCOSS Fall Leadership Summit. Available at: http://usny.nysed.gov/docs/presentations/nyscoss-fall-leadership-summit-2012.html.

Kingdon, J. (2011). *Agendas, Alternatives, and Public Policies, Updated 2nd edition.* New York: Longman.

Klein, M. M. (Ed.). (2005). *The Empire State: A History of New York.* Ithaca, NY: Cornell University Press.

Knipe, S., & Bottrell, C. (2023). Staffing Remote Schools: Perennial Failure. *Journal of Global Education and Research,* 7(2), 183–198.

Kolbe, T., Baker, B. D., Atchison, D., Levin, J., & Harris, P. (2021). The Additional Cost of Operating Rural Schools: Evidence from Vermont. *AERA Open,* 7, 2332858420988868.

Kozol, J. (2005). *The Shame of the Nation.* New York: Broadway Books.

Krippendorff, K. (1980). *Content Analysis*. New York: Sage Publications.
Kyricou, C. and P. Harriman. (1993). "Teacher Stress and School Merger." *School Organisation* 13.3, 297–302.
Kyvig, D. (2019). *Nearby History*. Lanham, MD: Rowman & Littlefield.
Labaree, D. (2008). *The Problem with Ed Schools*. New Haven, CT: Yale University Press.
Lamkin, M. (2006). "Challenges and Changes Faced by Rural Superintendents." *Rural Educator* 28(1), 17–25.
Lane, H. & L. O'Connor. (October 18, 2012). "Voters turn out in full-force for three-school merger vote." WKTV news downloaded from: http://www.wktv.com/news/local/Voters-turn-out-in-full-force-for-three-school-merger-vote-174802341.html
Langer, A. I., & Gruber, J. B. (2021). Political Agenda Setting in the Hybrid Media System: Why Legacy Media Still Matter a Great Deal. *The International Journal of Press/Politics*, 26(2), 313–340.
Lavalley, M. (2018). Out of the Loop: Rural Schools Are Largely Left out of Research and Policy Discussions, Exacerbating Poverty, Inequity, and Isolation. Alexandria, VA: Center for Public Education.
Lawson, H. A., Durand, F. T., Wilcox, K. C., Gregory, K. M., Schiller, K. S., & Zuckerman, S. J. (2017). "The Role of District and School Leaders' Trust and Communications in the Simultaneous Implementation of Innovative Policies. *Journal of School Leadership*, 27(1), 31–67.
Lee, J. et al. (2016). Consolidated as a Potential Cost Saving Measure for New Hampshire's Education System. PRS Policy Brief 1516-10. Nelson Rockefeller Center at Dartmouth Collge.
Leech, N. L., Haug, C. A., Rodriguez, E., & Gold, M. (2022). Why Teachers Remain Teaching in Rural Districts: Listening to the Voices from the Field. *The Rural Educator*, 43(3), 1–9.
Lennon, N. (2021). "Folks Like Us": Exploring State Education Policy in New York's Rural School Districts. (Doctoral dissertation, State University of New York at Albany).
Leo, A., Wilcox, K. C., & Yu, F. (2021). "An Ecological View of Rural Student Aspirations: Lessons from New York's North Country. *Rural Society*, 1–21.
Liebman, B. (2015). "Three Men in a Room" and Albany-Where Did the Phrase Come From? *Available at SSRN 2649989*.
Liu, X., et al. (2010). Understanding Local Policy Making: Policy Elites Perception of Local Agenda Setting and Alternative Policy Selection. *Policy Studies Journal* 38.(1), 69–91.
Livingston County News Editorial. (2012). "Are Rural Schools a Threatened Species?" Downloaded from: http://thelcn.com/2012/04/11/are-rural-schools-a-threatened-species/
Lobao, L., Gray, M., Cox, K., & Kitson, M. (2018). "The Shrinking State? Understanding the Assault on the Public Sector." *Cambridge Journal of Regions, Economy and Society*, 11(3), 389–408.
Loewen, J. W. (2021). "Foreword: A Connected Fringe." In *Neo-Confederacy*. Austin: University of Texas Press, ix–xii.

Longhurst, J. (2020). "A Rural Educator Responds to the Assault on the Capitol." *The Rural Educator*, 41(3), 55–56.

Lonneville, J. D. (2014). *Why Some School Districts Outperform Others: A Mixed-methods Study on Poverty, Student Performance on the New York State School Assessments, and School District Funding across Rural, Suburban, and Urban School Districts*. Lewiston, NY: Niagara University.

Loveland, F. (1993). Victor M. Rice and Andrew S. Draper: The Origins of Educational Centralization in Rural New York State. PhD Diss. State University of New York at Buffalo.

Lowenthal, D. (1998). *The Heritage Crusade and the Spoils of History.* Cambridge: Cambridge University Press.

Lucas, J. (2013). Exploring Structural Changes to Local ABCs in Three Provincial-Municipal Domains, 1800–2010. Paper given at Canadian Political Science Association.

Lundine, S. (2008). 21st Century Local Government. Albany, NY: New York State Commission on Local Government Efficiency and Competitiveness. Downloaded: http://www.nyslocalgov.org/report_page.asp

Lyson, T. (2002). "What Does a School Mean to a Community." *Journal of Research in Rural Education* 17.3, 131–137.

Macan, L. (2012). *Elementary School and Middle School Principals' Theories of Action in Two Rural School Districts*. PhD Diss, University at Albany.

Mann, B. (2022). Republicans Won House Seats in Blue New York. Those Wins Could Help Shape Congress. NPR: https://www.npr.org/2022/12/03/1139399457/republican-house-wins-new-york

Mantas-Kourounis, E. M. (2021). In the Trenches: The Local Politics of Civic Education (Doctoral dissertation, Columbia University).

Maranto, R. and J. Shuls. (2012). "How Do We Get Them on the Farm? Efforts to Improve Rural Teacher Recruitment and Retention in Arkansas." *Rural Educator* 41(1), 32–40.

Martin, J. & D. Meyerson. (1988). "Organizational Cultures and the Denial, Channeling and Acknowledgement of Ambiguity." In L. Pondy, Boland and Thomas, eds. *Managing Ambiguity and Change*. Hoboken, NJ: John Wiley and Sons, 93–125.

McDermott, K. (1999). *Controlling Public Education*. Lawrence, KS: University of Kansas Press.

McHenry-Sorber, E. (2009). "School Consolidation in Pennsylvania." *Beacon* 5.4.

McHenry-Sorber, E., & Campbell, M. P. (2019). "Teacher Shortage as a Local Phenomenon: District Leader Sensemaking, Responses, and Implications for Policy." *Education Policy Analysis Archives*, 27, 87–87.

McHenry-Sorber, E., & Schafft, K. A. (2015). 'Make My Day, Shoot a Teacher': tactics of inclusion and exclusion, and the contestation of community in a rural school–community conflict. *International Journal of Inclusive Education*, 19(7), 733–747.

McHenry-Sorber, E., & Sutherland, D. H. (2020). "Metaphors of Place-Conscious Leadership in the Multidistrict Superintendency: Negotiating Tensions of

Place-Consciousness and District-Wide Goal Attainment." *Journal of School Leadership*, 30(2), 105–126.

McLendon, M. & L. Cohen-Vogel. (2008). "Understanding Education Policy Change in the American States: Lessons from Political Science." In B. Cooper, et al., eds. *Handbook of Education Politics and Policy.* New York: Routledge, 30–51.

McMahon, E.J. (2011). "Empire State's Half Century Exodus: A Population Migration Overview." *Empire Center for New York State Policy Research Bulletin* 6.1

McMahon, E.J. and J. Barro. (2010). "A Blueprint for a Better Budget." Albany, NY: *Empire Center for New York State Policy.*

McMahon, E. (2020). "New York had Largest Population Decline 2019–2020 of Any State." *Empire Center for New York State Policy.*

Meier, E. (2012). "Heated Debate Erupts on Facebook Following Herkimer County School Merger Vote." http://lite987.com/heated-debate-erupts-on-facebook-following-herkimer-county-school-merger-vote/

Meinxer, C. (2012). "Piseco School Will Shut Its Door." *Hamilton County Express.* http://hamiltoncountyexpress.com/News/073112PisecoSchoolClosing

Meyer, et al. (1998). "Bureaucratization without Centralization." In L. Zucker, ed. *Institutional Papers and Organization.* Ballinger, 139–167. Downloaded from cornell.edu.

Michael, P. (2012). Testimony to the New New York Education Reform Commission. Available: http://www.governor.ny.gov/sites/governor.ny.gov/files/archive/assets/documents/MohawkValley9-24-12/DrPatrickMichelTestimony.pdf

Miller, L. (2012). "Situating the Rural Teacher Labor Market in the Broader Context: A Descriptive Analysis of the Market Dynamics in New York State." *Journal of Research in Rural Education* 27(13). Retrieved from: http://jrre.psu.edu/articles/27-12.pdf.

Miller, J. (2021). "Let's Not Do Anything Drastic!: Processes of Reproducing Rural Marginalization in Education Policy Decision-making." Paper Presented at the Rural Sociology Society Annual Meeting.

Mills, E. (2009). "A Tale of Two Towns: The Significance of a School to a Rural Community." *Journal of Inquiry and Action in Education* 2.2, 109–119.

Monk, D. H., & Haller, E. J. (1986). Organizational Alternatives for Small Rural Schools. Final Report to the Legislature of the State of New York.

Moon, N. (2012). "Assembly Doesn't Pass Regional High School Legislation. *Dunkirk Observer.* http://www.observertoday.com/page/content.detail/id/573569/Assembly-doesn-t-pass-regional-high-school-legislation.html?nav=5047

Mucciaroni, G. (1992). "The Garbage Can Model & the Study of Policymaking: A Critique." *Polity* 24.3, 459–482.

Mueller, J. T., McConnell, K., Burow, P. B., Pofahl, K., Merdjanoff, A. A., & Farrell, J. (2021). "Impacts of the COVID-19 Pandemic on Rural America." *Proceedings of the National Academy of Sciences*, 118(1), 2019378118.

Mullins, R., & Mullins, B. (2021). "Everybody Lives Near Appalachia: Examining Hillbilly Elegy's Impact on American Society." *Theory and Practice in Rural Education,* 11.2, 113–117

References

Murphy, J. (2022). *Your Children are Greatly in Danger.* Ithaca, NY: Cornell University Press.

Mykerezi, E., Kostandini, G., Jordan, J. L., & Melo, I. (2014). "On Rural-urban Differences in Human Capital Formation: Finding the 'Bottlenecks.'" *Journal of Rural Social Sciences*, 29(1), 2.

National Center for Educational Statistics (NCES). (2011/2022). *National Education Statistics.* Washington, DC.

New York Post. (2012). "Singin' the Tax Cap Blues." Downloaded from: http://nypost.com/2012/07/30/singin-tax-cap-blues/

New York State Board of Regents. (2012). "Report to the P-12 Committee." Downloaded from: www.nysed.gov

New York State Commission on Local Government Efficiencies. (2008). "21st Century Local Government." Downloaded from: http://www.nyslocalgov.org/pdf/LGEC_Final_Report.pdf?pagemode=bookmarks

New York State Commission on Property Tax Relief. (2008). "A Preliminary Report of Findings and Recommendations." Downloaded from http://blog.syracuse.com/indepth/2008/06/Suozzi%20report

New York State Office of the Comptroller. (2011). Local Government and School Accountability Laws of 2011. Downloaded from: http://www.osc.state.ny.us/localgov/realprop/

New York State Education Department. (1956). *Master Plan for School District Reorganization in New York State.* Albany: The University of the State of New York. www.ocmboces.org/tfiles/folder1613/1958masterplanPartA_I.pdf

New York State School Boards Association. (1947). "The Crises in Central School Finance." Albany, NY: Author.

NYSSBA. (2013). To Merge or Not To Merge: Making Sense of School Mergers. Albany, NY: NY State School Boards Association.

NYSASBO. (2014). Why Do School Consolidations Fail? Albany, NY: Author. Downloaded: http://www.nysasbo.org/uploads/files/1398091412_NYSASBO%20School%20Merger%20Study%20April%202014%20(1).pdf

NYSED. (1947). Master Plan for School Reorganization. Albany NY.

NYSED. (1958). Master Plan for School Reorganization. Albany, NY: Author

NYSOSC. (2007). 2007 Annual Report on Local Governments. Albany, NY: Office of State Comptroller.

New York State Archives. School District Reorganization Series. B0472-84 B4 F1.

NYS Office of State Comptroller. (2009). Making the Grade: Five Years of School District Accountability. Albany, NY: Author. Available: http://nassaucivic.com/sda09.pdf

NYSED. (N.D.). *Guide to the Reorganization of School Districts.* Available: http://www.p12.nysed.gov/mgtserv/sch_dist_org/GuideToReorganizationOfSchoolDistricts.htm

NYSED. (2014). State Accountability System. Downloaded: www.nysed.gov/p12

NYSED. (2015). New York State Student Information Reporting System Manual (version 11.6). Albany, NY: Author. downloaded: http://www.p12.nysed.gov/irs/sirs/documents/2015-16SIRSManual11-6.pdf

NYSOSC. (N.D.) Board of Education Training https://www.osc.state.ny.us/localgov/training/modules/myfp/reserves.htm

NYSSBA. (2014). The Perils of the Proposed Property Tax Freeze. Albany, NY: Author.

New York Times Editorial. (March 26, 2011). "Rich District, Poor District." *New York Times.* downloaded from: http://www.nytomes.com/3011/03/27/opinion/27sun1.html

Niccolai, A. R., Damaske, S., & Park, J. (2022). "We Won't Be Able to Find Jobs Here: How Growing Up in Rural America Shapes Decisions About Work." *RSF: The Russell Sage Foundation Journal of the Social Sciences* 8(4), 87–104.

Nitta, et al. (2010). "A Phenomenological Study of Rural School Consolidation." *Journal of Research in Rural Education* 25(2).

O'Connor, L. (2012). "Opinions Divided with School Merger Vote Two Days Away." WKTV news downloaded from: http://www.wktv.com/community/news/Opinions-divide-with-school-merger-vote-two-days-away--174511161.html

Opfer, D. (2011). "Defining and Identifying Hard to Staff Schools: The Role of School Demographics and Conditions." *Educational Administrative Quarterly* 47.4, 582–619.

OSC. (2006). Sullivan West. Downloaded: www.osc.state.ny.us/localgov/audits/2006/schools/sullivan.htm. Reported in Record Online 10/18/2006. recordonline.com/story/news/2006/10/18/state-local-school-district-wasted/S3035/97007/

O'Shea, C. M., & Zuckerman, S. J. (2022). "Comparing Rural and Non-rural Principal's Instructional Leadership in the Age of ESSA." *The Rural Educator* 43(3), 10–25.

Osterud, N. G. (2012). *Putting the Barn before the House*. Ithaca, NY: Cornell University Press.

Palmer, T. W. (2017). "New York State rural school superintendents' perceptions of their ability to fund instructional programs and advanced course offerings since the enactment of the property tax cap legislation of 2011." Sage Graduate School.

Panos, A., & Seelig, J. (2019). "Discourses of the Rural Rust Belt: Schooling, Poverty, and Rurality." *Theory & Practice in Rural Education* 9(1), 23.

Papacharissi, Z. (2004). "Democracy Online." *New Media and Society* 6.2.

Parkerson, D. & J. Parkerson. (2015). *Assessment, Bureaucracy, and Consolidation.* Lanham, MD: Rowman & Littlefield.

Parshall, L. (2019). "Dissolving Village Governments in New York State." *Policy Brief from Rockefeller Institute of Government, SUNY.* Link: https://rockinst.org/wp-content/uploads/2019/06/Dissolving-Village-Government-in-NYS.pdf

Parshall, L. (2023). *In Local Hands*. Albany, NY: SUNY Press.

Parsons, R. (2014). Putting Students First: Final Action Plan of the New New York Education Reform Commission. Downloaded from: http://www.governor.ny.gov/sites/governor.ny.gov/files/archive/assets/documents/NewNYEducationReformCommissionFinalActionPlan.pdf

Parton, C. (2023). *Country Teacher in City Schools.* Lanham, MD: Lexington Books.

Patrick, S. K., Grissom, J. A., Woods, S. C., & Newsome, U. W. (2021). "Broadband Access, District Policy, and Student Opportunities for Remote Learning During COVID-19 School Closures." *AERA Open* 7, 23328584211064298.

Patterns for Progress Hudson Valley. (2012). Closed Schools, Open Minds. Report available: http://pattern-for-progress.org/sites/default/files/SCHOOL%20REPORT%20FINAL.pdf

Peshkin, A. (1982). *The Imperfect Union.* Chicago: University of Chicago Press.

Peshkin, A. (1978). *Growing Up American* Chicago: University of Chicago Press.

Peters, S. J., & Morgan, P. A. (2004). The Country Life Commission: Reconsidering a Milestone in American Agricultural History. *Agricultural History* 289–316.

Piscitello, J., Kim, Y. K., Orooji, M., & Robison, S. (2022). "Sociodemographic Risk, School Engagement, and Community Characteristics: A Mediated Approach to Understanding High School Dropout." *Children and Youth Services Review* 133, 106347.

Ponterotto, J. G. (2006). "Brief Note on the Origins, Evolution, and Meaning of the Qualitative Research Concept Thick Description." *The Qualitative Report* 11(3), 538–549.

Population and Demographics. (2010). New York State Census Maps. Available from: http://pad.human.cornell.edu/maps2010/atlas.cfm

Prestipino, A. M. (2020). *Exploring the Role of Secondary Principal Leadership in Advancing the School Improvement Process* (Doctoral dissertation, Sage Graduate School).

Price, H. (2008). *Mobilizing the Community to Help Students Succeed.* Alexandria, VA: ASCD.

Pugh, T. (1994). "Rural School Consolidation in New York State, 1795–1993." PhD diss., Syracuse University.

QUESTAR III. (2010). 2010–2011 Executive Proposal for Aid to Education. Hudson, NY: Author. Downloaded: http://sap.questar.org/publications/budget/2010-11_Enacted_Budget.pdf

Rassmussen, T. (2009). *From Oxcart to Automobile.* Lanham, MD: University Press of America.

Ravitch, D. (2016). *The Death and Life of the Great American School System: How Testing and Choice are Undermining Education.* New York: Basic Books.

Reagan, E. M., Hambacher, E., Schram, T., McCurdy, K., Lord, D., Higginbotham, T., & Fornauf, B. (2019). "Place Matters: Review of the Literature on Rural Teacher Education." *Teaching and Teacher Education: An International Journal of Research and Studies* 80(1), 83–93.

Reardon, S. (2011). "The Widening Academic Achievement Gap between the Rich and the Poor: New Evidence and Possible Explanations." In Duncan and Murnane, eds. *Whither Opportunity: Rising Inequality, Schools and Children's Life Chances.* New York: Russell Sage Foundation, 91–116.

Reardon, S. and J. Robinson. (2008). "Patterns and Trends in Racial/Ethnic and Socioeconomic Academic Achievement Gaps." In H. Ladd and E. Fiske, eds. *Handbook of Research in Education Finance and Policy.* New York: Routledge, 497–516.

Reardon, S. F., & Yun, J. T. (2002). Private School Racial Enrollments and Segregation. Civil Rights Project. From Eric Database.

Rebell, M. (2011/2012). "Safeguarding the Right to a Sound Basic Education in times of Fiscal Constraint." *Albany Law Review* 75(4). 1855–1976.

Reilly, S. (2013). "School Mergers Lose to Local Pride." Downloaded from: http://www.shreveporttimes.com/article/CB/20131206/NEWS01/312060083/School-mergers-lose-local-pride

Reynolds, D. (1995). "Rural Education: Decentralizing the Consolidation Debate." In E. Castle, ed. *The Changing American Countryside*. Lawrence, KS: University Press of Kansas, 451–480.

Reynolds, D. (1999). *There Goes the Neighborhood*. Iowa City: University of Iowa Press.

Rey, J. C. (2014). "The Rural Superintendency and the Need for a Critical Leadership of Place. *Journal of School Leadership* 24(3).

Rhodes, M. et al. (2022). *Crush It From The Start: 50 Tips for New Teachers*. Orlando, FL: School Rubric.

Richter, D. K., & Merrell, J. H. (Eds.). (2010). *Beyond the Covenant Chain: The Iroquois and Their Neighbors in Indian North America, 1600–1800*. Penn State Press.

Rimando, M., Brace, A. M., Namageyo-Funa, A., Parr, T. L., Sealy, D. A., Davis, T. L., . . . & Christiana, R. W. (2015). "Data Collection Challenges and Recommendations for Early Career Researchers." *The Qualitative Report* 20(12), 2025–2036.

Rivervalley Press. (2015). http://www.salamancapress.com/news/plenty-of-nostalgia-in-former-little-valley-school/article_c9186002-c28b-11e4-a5cc-ebc198b429fb.html

Rock, A. and J. Tabor (2020). Home Tweet Home: Can Social Media Define a Community? *Journal of Appalachian Studies*, 26(1), 87–105.

Rodgers, J. et al. (2014). Easy Experiences Implementing Voluntary School District Mergers in Vermont. *Journal of Research in Rural Education*, 29(7), 1–14.

Romein, C. A., et al. (2020). State of the Field: Digital History. *History* 105(365), 291–312.

Ross, W. E. (1960). *A study of personnel factors affecting the morale status of teachers of two rural school systems in New York State and including comparisons of findings with those of a similar study completed for a New Jersey Suburban School System*. New York University.

Rousmaniere, K. (2013). "Those Who Can't Teach." *History of Education Quarterly* 53.1, 90–103.

Sageman, J. (2022). School Closures and Rural Population Decline. *Rural Sociology*, 87(2), 960–92.

Saldana, J. (2021). *The Coding Manual for Qualitative Researchers*. New York: Sage.

Sansouci, J. (2007). *An Examination of Selected Job Factors that Influence New York State Rural School Superintendents to Voluntarily Exit Their Superintendency*. EdD. Diss. University of Rochester, NY.

Schafft, K. (2006). "Poverty, Residential Mobility, and Student Transiency within a Rural New York School District." *Rural Sociology* 71.2.

Schafft, K. A. (2016). "Rural Education as Rural Development: Understanding the Rural School–Community Well-being Linkage in a 21st-century Policy Context." *Peabody Journal of Education* 91(2), 137–154.

Schafft, K. & Jackson, A. (Eds.), (2010). "Rural Education for the Twenty-first Century: Identity, Place, and Community in a Globalizing World." University Park, PA: Penn State University Press.

Schein, E. (1990). "Organizational Culture." *American Psychologist* 45, 109–119.

Schemmel, A. (2022). Anti-CRT School Board Candidates Look for Wins across NY State. *WHAM.* https://13wham.com/news/local/anti-crt-school-board-candidates-in-ny-look-for-wins-across-the-state-crircal-race-theory-new-york-1776-project

Schmuck, R. & P. Schmuck. (1992). *Small Districts, Big Problems.* Newbury Park, CA: Corwin Press.

Schneider, J., & Gottlieb, D. (2021). In Praise of Ordinary Measures: The Present Limits and Future Possibilities of Educational Accountability. *Educational Theory* 71(4), 455–473.

Schneider, J. (2018). *Beyond Test Scores.* Cambridge, MA: Harvard University Press.

Schneider, J., & Berkshire, J. (2020). *A Wolf at the Schoolhouse Door: The Dismantling of Public Education and the Future of School.* New York: The New Press.

School Merger Study Survey Results. (ND). Downloaded from: http://www.ilioncsd.org/District/MergerStudy/ThreeSchool/CombinedSurveyResults.pdf

Schulte, A. & B. Walker-Gibbs, eds. (2016). *Self Studies in Rural Teacher Education.* New York: Springer.

Schwartz, A. et al. (2011). "Do Small Schools Improve Performance in Large, Urban Districts?" NYU School Working Paper 4–11. Downloaded from: http://steinhardt.nyu.edu/scmsAdmin/media/users/qd217/Working_Paper_04-11.pdf)

Scott, C. (2009). "Improving Low-Performing Schools: Lessons from Five Years of Studying School Restructuring Under No Child Left Behind." *Center on Education Policy.*

Scott, J. (1990). *Domination and the Arts of Resistance.* New Haven, CT: Yale University Press.

Scribner, C. F. (2016). *The Fight for Local Control.* Ithaca, NY: Cornell University Press.

See, B. H., Morris, R., Gorard, S., & El Soufi, N. (2020). "What Works in Attracting and Retaining Teachers in Challenging Schools and Areas?" *Oxford Review of Education* 46(6), 678–697.

Seelig, J. L. (2021). "Place Anonymization as Rural Erasure? A Methodological Inquiry for Rural Qualitative Scholars." *International Journal of Qualitative Studies in Education* 34(9), 857–870.

Seelig, J. L., & McCabe, K. M. (2021). "Why Teachers Stay: Shaping a New Narrative on Rural Teacher Retention." *Journal of Research in Rural Education* 37(8).

Self, T. (2001a). "A Post Consolidation Evaluation." Paper presented at the Annual meeting of the Mid-Western Educational Research Association.

Self, T. (2001b). "Evaluation of a Single School District Consolidation in Ohio." *American Secondary Education* 30.1.

Sergiovanni, T. (1994). *Building Community in Schools.* San Francisco, CA: Jossey Bass.

SES Study Team. 2011. "A Reorganization Feasibility Study on Behalf of the Frankfort-Schuyler, Herkimer, Ilion and Mohawk Central School Districts." http://images.bimedia.net/documents/ReorganizationStudy.pdf

Sharp, T. (2012). "Two Niagara County Superintendents Oversee Two Districts Each." *Buffalo News.* Downloaded: http://www.buffalonews.com/city-region/niagara-county/two-niagara-county-superintendents-oversee-two-districts-each-20131109

Sher, J. P., & Tompkins, R. B. (1976). *Economy, Efficiency, and Equality: The Myths of Rural School and District Consolidation.* Washington, DC: The National Institute of Education.

Sherman, J. (2021). *Dividing Paradise: Rural Inequality and the Diminishing American Dream.* Berkley: University of California Press.

Sherman, J. & R. Sage. (2011). "Sending Off all of Your Good Treasures." *Journal of Research in Rural Education* 26.11.

Sherman, J., & Schafft, K. A. (2022). "'Turning Their Back on Kids': Inclusions, Exclusions, and the Contradictions of Schooling in Gentrifying Rural Communities." *RSF: The Russell Sage Foundation Journal of the Social Sciences* 8(3), 150–170.

Shober, A. (2012). "Governors Make the Grade: Growing Gubernatorial Influence in State Education Policy." *Peabody Journal of Education* 87, 559–575.

Simonelli, J. (2014). "Home Rule and Natural Gas Development in New York: Civil Fracking Rights." *Journal of Political Ecology* 21(1), 258–278.

Sipple, J. et al. (2004). "Stalking Cost Effective Practices in Rural Schools." *Journal of Education Finance* 29.3, 237–256.

Sipple, J. W., Francis, J. D., & Fiduccia, P. C. (2019). "Exploring the Gradient: The Economic Benefits of 'Nearby' Schools on Rural Communities." *Journal of Rural Studies* 68, 251–263.

Sipple, J. (n.d.). The New York State Center for Rural Schools. Cornell University. Accessed: http://www.nyruralschools.org/

Sipple, J., et al. (2004). "Adoption and Adaptation: School District Responses to State Imposed Learning and Graduation Requirements." *Educational Evaluation and Policy Analysis* 26(2), 143–168. Retrieved from http://www.jstor.org/stable/3699557

Sipple, J. W., & Yao, Y. (2015). "The Unequal Impact of the Great Recession on the Instructional Capacity of Rural Schools." In Williams & Grooms, eds. *Educational Opportunity in Rural Contexts: The Politics of Place.* Charlotte, NC: IAP.

Slentz, K. (2011). Remarks to the Staff of the Office of Instructional Support and Development. Internal NYSED meeting.

Smarsh, S. (2018). *Heartland.* New York: Scribner.

Smith, P. (1999). "'It's Déjà vu All Over Again': The Rural School Problem Revisited." In D. Chalker, Ed. *Leadership for Rural Schools: Lessons for All Educators.* Lancaster, PA: Technomic Publishing Co., Inc., 25–62.

Snyder, D. (1998). Voters Reject Merger of School Districts. *Buffalo News November 18, 1998.*

Sorrell-White, S. (10/10/12). "Opinions Vary on Proposed Herkimer County School Merger." Utica Observer Dispatch available from: http://www.uticaod.com/news/x772636693/Opinions-vary-on-proposed-Herkimer-County-school-merger

Spaulding, F.T. (1967). The Addresses and Papers of Francis Trow Spaulding. Albany: University of the State of New York and the New York State Education Department.

Sperry, S. & P. Hill. (2015). The Politics of Education in Small Rural School Districts. Boise, ID: Rural Opportunities Coalition of Idaho. Downloaded: http://www.rociidaho.org/wp-content/uploads/2015/01/ROCI_2014_K-12Politics_FINAL.pdf

Spring, J. (1997). *American Education.* Oxford: Routledge.

Stake, R. (1995). *The Art of the Case Study.* New York: Sage.

Stanley, L. et al. (2008). "School Adjustment in Rural and Urban Communities." *Journal of Youth Adolescence* 37, 225–238.

Steffes, T. (2008). "Solving the 'Rural School Problem.'" *History of Education Quarterly* 48(2). 181–220.

Steele. J. (2010). The Leadership Role of the Superintendent in a Time Of Change and Scarce Resources: A Qualitative Study of Three School District Reorganization Efforts. EdD. Diss, Russell Sage Graduate College.

Stein, A., & Daniels, J. (2017). *Going Public: A Guide for Social Scientists.* Chicago, IL: University of Chicago Press.

Stone, D. (1989). "Causal Stories and the Formation of Policy Agendas." *Political Science Quarterly* 104(2), 281–300.

Strange, M. (2011). "Finding Fairness for Rural Students." *Phi Delta Kappa Magazine* 92(6), 8–15.

Sunderman, G. L., Coghlan, E., & Mintrop, R. (2017). School Closure as a Strategy to Remedy Low Performance. *National Education Policy Center.*

Suozzi, T. (2008). A Preliminary Report of the Findings and Recommendations to Governor David A. Patterson. Albany: *New York State Commission on Property Tax Relief.*

Sutherland, D., McHenry-Sorber, E., & Willingham, J. N. (2022). "Just Southern: Navigating the Social Construction of a Rural Community in the Press for Educational Equity. *The Rural Educator,* 43(1), 37–53.

Szuberla, C., VanDeventer, S., Cunningham, D., & Thurnau, C. (2002). School District Responses to Building Aid Incentives. Research Monograph.

Tangorra, C. (2013). The Programmatic, Financial, and Cultural Impact of Failed School District Reorganization Efforts: Perspectives of School Leadership Teams. Ed.D. Diss, Russell Sage Graduate College.

Taylor, A. (2002). *American Colonies: The Settling of North America (The Penguin History of the United States, Volume 1).* New York: Penguin.

Teisman, G. R. (2000), "Models For Research into Decision-Making Processes: On Phases, Streams and Decision-Making Rounds." *Public Administration,* 78: 937–956.

The Rural School and Community Trust. (2009). Why Rural Matters 2009. Arlington, VA: Author. Available: www.ruraledu.org/whyruralmatters.

Theobald, P. (1997). *Teaching the Commons.* Boulder, CO: Westview Press.

Theobald, P. (2017). "Hillbilly Elegy: A Memoir of a Family and Culture in Crisis." *Journal of Research in Rural Education (Online)*, 32(8), 1–3.

Theobald, P. & A. Alsmeyer. (1995). "Cultural Obstacles on the Road to Rural Educational Renewal." *Education and Culture* 12.2.

Theobald, P. & K. Wood. (2010). "Learning to Be Rural." In Schafft & Armstrong, eds. *Rural Education for the 21st Century.* University Park, PA: Pennsylvania State University Press, 17–33.

Theobald, P. (1995). *Call School.* Carbondale, IL: Southern Illinois Press.

Thier, M., Longhurst, J. M., Grant, P. D., & Hocking, J. E. (2021). "Research Deserts: A Systematic Mapping Review of US Rural Education Definitions and Geographies." *Journal of Research in Rural Education (Online)*, 37(2), 1–24.

Thier, M., Beach, P., Martinez Jr, C. R., & Hollenbeck, K. (2020). "Take Care When Cutting: Five Approaches to Disaggregating School Data as Rural and Remote." *Theory & Practice in Rural Education*, 10(2), 63–84.

Thier, M., & Beach, P. (2019). "Stories We Don't Tell: Research's Limited Accounting of Rural Schools." *School Leadership Review* 14(2), 5.

Thomas, A. R. (2005). *Gilboa: New York's Quest for Water and the Destruction of a Small Town.* Lanham, MD: University Press of America.

Thomas, A. R. (2003). *In Gotham's Shadow: Globalization and Community Change in Central New York.* Albany, NY: SUNY Press.

Thomas, A. R., & Smith, P. J. (2009). *Upstate Down: Thinking about New York and Its Discontents.* Lanham, MD: University Press of America.

Tieken, M. C. (2014). *Why Rural Schools Matter.* Chapel Hill: University of North Carolina Press.

Tieken, M. C., & Auldridge-Reveles, T. R. (2019). "Rethinking the School Closure Research: School Closure as Spatial Injustice." *Review of Educational Research* 89(6), 917–953.

Tieken, M. C., & Montgomery, M. K. (2021). "Challenges Facing Schools in Rural America." *State Education Standard* 21(1), 6–11.

Tierney, W. (1988). "Organizational Culture: Defining the Essentials." *Journal of Higher Education* 59, 2–21

Timbs, R. (1997). Implications of Reorganization Aid in New York State. Unpublished PhD. Diss. Syracuse University.

Times Union (2014). "Editorial: One Less Authority? Sure." *The Albany Times Union.* Available at: http://www.timesunion.com/opinion/article/Editorial-One-less-authority-Sure-5502934.php

Topix Forum BOASF: http://www.topix.com/forum/city/herkimer-ny/T5233IU2SAQSBOASF/p5

Topix Forum C42F1: http://www.topix.com/forum/city/herkimer-ny/T8BV8lON0o6C42F1

Topix Forum JEFRU: http://www.topix.com/forum/city/herkimer-ny/TSOUKK7F7QO4JEFRU

Topix Forum NIIHU5: http://www.topix.com/forum/city/herkimer-ny/TCNOOHI2FL2NIIHU5

Topix Forum HEO9I: http://www.topix.com/forum/city/herkimer-ny/TBF6G15U5MI0HEO9I

Topix Forum SOCQ: http://www.topix.com/forum/city/herkimer-ny/T27NAAT1I68LSOCQ6

Topix Forum U76TU: http://www.topix.com/forum/city/herkimer-ny/T3S0QAAC63AIU76TU/p8

Topix Forum 712IE: http://www.topix.com/forum/city/herkimer-ny/T0905IV8L280712IE

Topix Forum RDNH4: http://www.topix.com/forum/city/herkimer-ny/T6LB6RDQOCRMRDHNH4

Topix Forum RL69P0: http://www.topix.com/forum/city/herkimer-ny/TQ14M1858C4CLR6P0

Topix Forum SOCQ: http://www.topix.com/forum/city/herkimer-ny/T27NAAT1I68LSOCQ6

Topix Forum U76TI: http://www.topix.com/forum/city/herkimer-ny/T3S0QAAC63AIU76TU/p8

Tracy, K. (2010). *Challenges of Ordinary Democracy.* University Park, PA: Pennsylvania State University Press.

Tran, H., Hardie, S., Gause, S., Moyi, P., & Ylimaki, R. (2020). "Leveraging the Perspectives of Rural Educators to Develop Realistic Job Previews for Rural Teacher Recruitment and Retention." *The Rural Educator* 41(2), 31–46.

Trujillo, K. (2022). "Rural Identity as a Contributing Factor to Anti-intellectualism in the US." *Political Behavior* 44(3), 1509–1532.

Tuttle, B. (2015). "8 Reasons Your Property Taxes Are So Damn High." *Fortune Magazine.* downloaded from: http://fortune.com/2015/04/20/8-reasons-your-property-taxes-are-so-damn-high/

Tyack, D. B. (1972). "The Tribe and the Common School: Community Control in Rural Education." *American Quarterly* 24(1), 3–19.

Tyack, D. and L. Cuban. (1997). *Tinkering Towards Utopia.* Harvard: Harvard University Press.

Unadilla Valley. (2013). Unadilla Valley Celebrates 10 Years in Consolidated School. http://www.uvstorm.org/protected/ArticleView.aspx?iid=42U20&dasi=3YI0

USDOE. (2011). Guidance on School Restructuring. Downloaded: https://oese.ed.gov/tag/school-restructuring/

USDOE. (2010). Teacher Improvement Fund. Downloaded from: http://cecr.ed.gov/TIFgrantees/list.cfm

Upstate United. (2022). New York is Taxed Out. https://upstateunited.com/2021/04/28/new-taxed-out-fact-sheet-examines-new-yorks-historic-tax-hikes/

Vance, J. D. (2016). *Hillbilly Elegy.* New York, NY: HarperCollins.

Vance, J. D. (2018). *Hillbilly Elegy: A Memoir of a Family and Culture in Crisis.* HarperCollins.

Vazzana, C. M., & Rudi-Polloshka, J. (2019). "Appalachia Has Got Talent, but Why Does It Flow Away? A Study on the Determinants of Brain Drain from Rural USA." *Economic Development Quarterly* 33(3), 220–233.

Velasquez, A. (2012). "Social Media and On-line Political Discussion." *New Media and Society* 14.8.

Vergari, S. (2009). "New York." In Fusarelli, B. and B. Cooper, eds. *The Rising State: How State Power is Transforming our Nation's Schools.* Albany, NY: SUNY, 65–88.

Viteritti, J. (2001). "The Tip of the Iceberg: SURR Schools and Academic Failure in New York City." *Manhattan Institute for Policy Research.* Available at: http://www.manhattan-institute.org/html/cr_16.htm

Walker-Gibbs, B., Ludecke, M., & Kline, J. (2018). "Pedagogy of the Rural as a Lens for Understanding Beginning Teachers' Identity and Positionings in Rural Schools." *Pedagogy, Culture & Society*, 26(2), 301–314.

Wallace, M. L. (1996). *Mickey Mouse History and Other Essays on American Memory.* (Vol. 79). Temple University Press.

Wallin, D. (2007). "Policy Window or Hazy Dream"? *Canadian Journal of Educational Administration and Policy* 63.

Wallner, J. (2014). *Learning to School.* Toronto: University of Toronto Press.

Ward, J. and F. Rink. (1992). "Analysis of Stakeholder Opposition to School District Consolidation." *Journal of Research in Rural Education* 8:2, 11–19.

Warner, W., et al. (2010). "Micropolitics, Community Identity and School Consolidation." *Journal of School Public Relations* 21, 303–318.

Warren, M. (1999). *Democracy and Trust.* Cambridge: University of Cambridge Press.

Watertown Daily Times. (2014).

Weeks, K. et al., (2002). "States and Education." *Encyclopedia of Education.* Retrieved October 24, 2015, from Encyclopedia.com: http://www.encyclopedia.com/doc/1G2-3403200585.html

Weis, L. (1990). *Working Class without Work.* London: Routledge.

White, S. & M. Corbett, eds. (2014). *Doing Educational Research in Rural Settings.* New York: Routledge.

White, S., & Reid, J. (2008). "Placing Teachers? Sustaining Rural Schooling through Placeconsciousness in Teacher Education." *Journal of Research in Rural Education* 23(7), 1–11.

Wiles, D. (1994). "What Is Useful Policy Information in School Consolidation Debates?" *Journal of Education Finance* 19, 292–318.

Williams, S. M. (2013). "Micropolitics and Rural School Consolidation: The Quest for Equal Educational Opportunity in Webster Parish." *Peabody Journal of Education*, 88(1), 127–138.

Williams, S., & Tieken, M. C. (2021). "Commentary: Times Article on Rural School Misses Half the Story—Educational Success." *The Rural Educator*, 42(3), 72–73.

Willis, P. (1977). *Learning to Labor: How Working Class Kids Get Working Class Jobs (Morningside Edition 1981).* New York: Columbia University Press.

Winerip, M. (2011). "Tiny Town Recruits Students World Wide." *New York Times.* http://www.nytimes.com/2011/06/13/nyregion/tiny-newcomb-ny-recruits-students-worldwide.html?pagewanted=all

Winner, G. (2006). A Vision for Rural New York. Albany, NY: New York State Legislative Commission on Rural Resources. Downloaded from: RNYI.cornell.edu

White, S. and J. Reid. (2008). "Placing Teachers? Sustaining Rural Schooling through Place-consciousness in Teacher Education." *Journal of Research in Rural Education* 23(7). Retrieved from jrre.psu.edu/articles/23-7.pdf

WKTV Sports. (August 22, 2012). "School Merger: Football Athletes Speak about Proposed Merger." http://www.wktv.com/sports/Football-athletes-speak-about-proposed-merger-167104035.html

Woodrum, A. (2004). "State-mandated Testing and Cultural Resistance in Appalachian Schools." *Journal of Research in Rural Education* 19(1). Retrieved from http://www.umaine.edu/jrre/19-1.pdf.

Woodward, K. S. (1986). The Impact of Reorganization on School District Governance and Political Participation in a Centralized, Rural, New York State School District. Doctoral dissertation, Cornell University.

Wuthnow, R. (2018). *The Left Behind*. Princeton, NJ: Princeton University Press.

Yarger, K. D. (2018). *Cultural, Personal, and Professional Supports and Obstacles Affecting the Rural Superintendency* (Doctoral dissertation, Northcentral University).

Yinger, J. (Ed.). (2020). *Poverty And Proficiency: The Cost Of And Demand For Local Public Education*. Singapore: World Scientific.

Young, T. et al. (2010). "Understanding Agenda Setting in State Educational Policy." *Education Policy Analysis Archives* 18.15. Retrieved: http://epaa.asu.edu/ojs/article/view/771.

Zimmerle, J. C., & Lambert, C. (2019). "Globally Connected: Using Twitter to Support Rural Preservice Teachers." *Theory & Practice in Rural Education*, 9(1), 91–104.

Zimmerman, J. 2009. *Small Wonder: The Little Red School House in History and Memory*. New Haven, CT: Yale University Press.

Zimmer, T. et al. (2009). "Examining Economies of Scale in School Consolidations: Assessment of Indiana School Districts." *Journal of Educational Finance* 35(2), 103–127.

Zuckerman, S. J., Wilcox, K. C., Durand, F. T., Lawson, H. A., & Schiller, K. S. (2018). "Drivers for Change: A Study of Distributed Leadership and Performance Adaptation during Policy Innovation Implementation." *Leadership and Policy in Schools* 17(4), 618–646.

Zuckerman, S. J. (2019). Making Sense of Place: A Case Study of a Sensemaking in a Rural School-community Partnership. Unpublished dissertation, State University of New York, Albany.

Zuckerman, S. J. (2020). "'Why Can't This Work Here?': Social Innovation and Collective Impact in a Micropolitan Community." *Community Development*, 51(4), 401–419.

Index

accountability measures, 8–9, 13–14, 21–26, 67
Adequate Yearly Progress (AYP) measures, 13, 85, 87
administrators: recruitment and turnover as indicators, 24–25; salary discussions in the Herkimer County case study, 43–44; and teacher retention, 80–81; use of comparisons, 31
agenda setting theory, 10, 51; Diffusion Model, 17; Multiple Streams Model, 13, 14–15, 17–34; overview, 15; Phase Model, 15–16; Punctuated Equilibrium, 16; Rounds Model, 17
Algonquians people, 105
Alsbury, T., 86
Alsmeyer, A., 23
American Recovery and Reinvestment Act (ARRA), 68, 70
Anthony-Stevens, V., 4
Appalachian Regional Commission (ARC), 52, 65, 78, 80, 93
assessment, as an indicator, 22
Auldridge-Reveles, T. R., 93
autoethnography, 6, 19, 51, 116
Azano, A. P., 78, 89, 96

Baumgartner, F., 16, 17, 33

Beach, P., 5
Berry, C., 86–87
Biddle, C., 96, 107
Biden, Joe, 1
Biden administration, 47
Bill & Melinda Gates Foundation, 68
Binghamton University, 106
Board of Cooperative Education Services (BOCES), 30, 56–57, 61, 63, 70, 72, 80
Board of Regents, 63, 64
boards of education: feedback sources, 27–30; membership stability as indicator, 25; in the state merger process, 37–39
Brocton Central School District. *See* Brocton-Westfield case study
Brocton-Westfield case study: community description, 52–53; community discussions, 53–56; economics and money discussions, 53; media reporting, 56–57; policy stream, 55–56; political stream, 55–56; trust, lack of, 54
Brown, D., 8
budgets, 25–26
Bush, George W., 67

Cairney, P., 32–33

Campaign for Fiscal Equity, 39
Campbell, M. P., 79
Campbell-Halfaker, D. C., 84
Carr, P., 23, 65, 93
Catskill Rural Project, 62
Cattaraugus School District case study, 19–20, 56
Catte, E., 2, 108
Cervone, J. A., 5, 107
Chamberlin, J., 112
Chautauqua County. *See* Brocton-Westfield case study
Chiles, R., 60
Churchill, C., 102
Clark, S., 7
Cobb, R., 16, 17
community colleges, 106
community members: consolidation impacts, 11; as feedback source, 27–28; role of in educational reform, 82–84; in the state merger process, 37–39. *See also* rural communities
community study, 2
comparisons, 30–32
consolidation: agenda setting theory, 14–15; author's experiences, 19–20; Brocton-Westfield case study, 52–57; Cattaraugus School District case study, 19–20, 56; community impacts of, 11; defined, 14; Herkimer County case study, 10–11, 35, 40–49; historically, 61–63, 96–97, 117; identity as reason for defeat, 35–37; and improved educational opportunities, 85–87; increased expenditures, 84–85; leadership calls for, 9, 11, 13, 63–66; Leatherstocking failure, 88–89; lessons learned, 101–3; Little Valley Central School District case study, 6, 19–20, 56, 113; Magical Mountains Central School District case study, 97–98; Master Plan for School Reorganization, 19–20, 41, 61–62, 88, 116; media reporting, 35–36; Mountainside-Creekside case study, 98–99; research on, 19–20; state mandated, 37–39, 46; successful, 87–88; Timberline School District case study, 99–101; as an urban normative approach, 90–91
Contract for Excellence, 69
Corbett, M, 3, 4, 5, 23, 65, 82, 89, 90, 93, 95
Cordova, R. A., 84
Cornell University, 19, 106
COVID-19 pandemic, 9–10, 46–47, 56–57, 65, 70, 72–73, 76, 88, 111, 113
Cramer, K. J., 2, 8, 36, 77, 102, 107, 108, 111
Creekside Central School District. *See* Mountainside-Creekside case study
Critical Race Theory conflicts, 77, 113
Cubberley, Ellwood, 60, 108
Cuomo, Andrew, 39–40, 63–64, 110
Curtain, John, 67

Daniels, J., 112
Davidson, O., 78
Dearing, J., 33
demographic information, as an indicator, 22–23
desegregation, 67
DeYoung, A., 80, 95
discourse analysis, 36, 51
distant rural territory, 14
diversity, 4
Doukas, D., 41, 80, 108
Draper, Andrew Solan, 96, 108
Duncan, C., 5, 48, 80, 108
Duncombe, W., 20

economic advancement, schooling and, 78
education: accountability measures, 8–9, 13–14, 67; adequate, defining, 13–14; funding for, 37, 39–40, 63–64, 69–70; opportunities improved by consolidation, 85–87;

policies, 64–65; reforms, 9; urban school policy, 66–69. *See also* rural schools and education
Elder, C., 16, 17
elections, presidential, 1, 10, 108, 110
elites: and mass decision makers, 16; in rural communities, 8, 90
Ellis, R., 40, 42, 51, 90, 105
Elmira College, 106
Essert, P., 36, 61–62
ethnography, 8
Evans, R., 102
Every Student Succeeds Act (ESSA), 13, 59, 68, 72
Ewing, E., 93

feedback, 21, 27–30
fiscal monitoring, 29
Fischel, W., 77
Fitchen, J., 80, 93
Florida, Richard, 102
focusing events/crises/symbols, 21, 26–27
Folts, J. D., 60
fringe rural territory, 14
Fulkerson, G. M., 1, 105, 107, 112, 116

Gallo, J., 78
Gap Elimination Adjustment (GEA), 25–26, 39, 63
Gee, J. P., 36, 51
Gereluk, D., 4
Goodlad, J. L., 95
Gordon, N., 85
government, state: calls for consolidation by, 9, 11, 13; as feedback source, 29–30
graduation rates, as an indicator, 23
Grant, Philip, 107
Great Recession (2008), 11, 13, 37, 76, 99
Green, T., 93
Gregor, M. A., 84

Haller, E. J., 96

Hamilton County, 77–78
Haudenosaunee people, 105
heritage, 2
Herkimer County case study: Central School District, 41; community amenities and demographics, 40–41; consolidation defeat, 10–11, 35, 48–49; economics and money discussions, 43–45; identity discussions, 42–43; program discussions, 45; research process, 41–42; state mandate discussions, 45–47; study limitations, 47–48; trust, lack of, 43, 45–46, 48
Hibbard, M., 27
hidden narratives, 8
History of the University of the State of New York and the State Education Department (Folts), 60
Hochul, Kathy, 81
Hocking, Jessica, 107
Howard, R., 36, 61–62
Howlett, M., 33
Howley, A., 96
Howley, C., 2, 40, 96

indicators, 21–26
internet access, lack of, 10, 69, 80
Ithaca College, 106

Jackson, A., 23, 93
Jacobs, N., 102
January 6, 2021 riots, 1, 4, 108, 111
Johnson, A., 6
Jones, B., 16, 17
Jones, M., 32–33
Journal of Research in Rural Education (periodical), 107
Justice, B., 46

Kefalas, M., 23, 65, 93
King, John B., Jr., 64, 96
Kingdon, J., 10, 13, 14–15, 17–21, 31, 32–33, 40, 51, 116–17
Knight, B., 85

Kozol, J., 66
Kyvig, D., 36, 105

Langford, S., 4
Leatherstocking consolidation failure, 88–89
Leech, N. L., 78
Little Valley Central School District case study, 6, 19–20, 56, 113
Longhurst, J., 47, 107, 108
Lowenthal, D., 2
Lundine Commission, 63, 76
Lyson, T., 11, 51, 93

Macan, L., 19
Magical Mountains Central School District case study, 97–98
McCabe, K. M., 78
McHenry-Sorber, E., 79, 107
media: comparisons of indicators by, 31; consolidation reporting, 35–36; education spending reporting, 76–77; as feedback source, 28–29; role of in policy window, 33
merged, problematic use of term, 14
Miller, J., 11, 65, 93, 95, 112
Monk, D. H., 96
Mountainside-Creekside case study, 98–99
Mucciaroni, G., 32
Multiple Streams Model of agenda setting theory, 13, 14–15; comparisons, 21, 30–32; consolidation application, 19–20; critiques of, 32–34; feedback, 21, 27–30; focusing events/crises/symbols, 21, 26–27; indicators, 21–26; policy entrepreneur role, 18; policy stream, 17–18; policy window, 18; politics stream, 17–18; problem stream, 17–18, 20–26
Munis, K., 102
Murphy, J., 67

National Center for Education Statistics (NCES), 4, 14, 94
"nearby history" approach, 36
Newcomb, New York, 71
New York: economic struggles and school funding, 39; hydrofracking, 110; Master Plan for School Reorganization, 19–20, 41, 61–62, 88, 116; as a role model, 11; rural schools in, 94–96, 117; secessionists, 110; state merger process, 37–39, 46; uniqueness of, 105–13, 118; upstate/downstate narrative, 108–10; urban school policy, 66–69
New York Safe Act, 110
New York State Center for Rural Schools, 4
New York State Council of School Superintendents, 64
New York State Department of State, 37
New York State Education Department (NYSED), 14, 22, 25, 29–30, 37, 38, 60, 61, 68, 96, 116
New York State School Boards Association, 64
New York Times (periodical), 70, 77–78, 94
Nitta, K., 20, 86
No Child Left Behind (NCLB), 13, 67, 83, 85, 87
Northern Tennessee Army of the Confederacy flag, 1–2
nostalgic trap, 7–8
Nyquist, Ewald, 66

Office of Accountability (OA), 29
Office of the State Comptroller (OSC), 29
Olean Times Herald (periodical), 71–72

Palmer, T. W., 66
Panos, A., 7
parents, role of in educational reform, 82–84
Parkerson, D., 96

Parkerson, J., 96
Parshall, L., 51, 109
Parton, C., 89, 112
performance gap, 70
personal stories as focusing symbols, 27
Peshkin, A., 95, 101
Piseco, New York, 71
Ponterotto, J. G., 7
Pressman, J., 40
programmatic review, 29–30
property taxes, 63, 76, 95
Pugh, T., 95

Quality Improvement Plan (QIP), 30

Race to the Top, 13, 59, 68, 70
Rapp-Couldet Commission, 61
Raquette Lake, New York, 71
Rasmussen, T., 99
Reardon, S. F., 67
Redding, S., 2
remote rural territory, 14
reorganization, 14, 35–37, 59. *See also* consolidation
Rey, J. C., 8
Reynolds, W. M., 84, 95, 108
The Rise of the Creative Class (Florida), 102
Rochester City School District, 67–68
Rogers, E., 33
Romein, C. A., 41
rural, defined, 3, 4–5, 14
rural communities: COVID-19 pandemic effects on, 73; deficit narrative, 107–8, 111–12; demographics, 77–78; effects of urbanormativity, 1–2; elites in, 8; harmony trope, 5; identity of, 36–37; narratives about, 7–8; Northeastern United States, 3–4; outmigration from, 93; research on, 3; schools as the heart of, 51, 95; upstate/downstate narrative, 108–10; values of, 82–83

Rural School and Community Trust, 79–80
rural schools and education: accountability measures, 8–9; author's experiences, 6–10, 115–16; challenges, 75, 91; as community centers, 79–80; economics of, 76–79; historically, 59–63; historiography of, 4; indicators for, 21–26; infrastructural barriers facing, 79–81; loss of state aid for, 69–70; narratives about, 112–13; in New York state, 94–96, 117; reform pushback by communities, 81–84; research on, 2–6; restructuring of, 71–73; as a wicked problem, 89–91, 117
rural-urban divide, 6–7

Sage, R., 23, 80
Sageman, J., 81
Saldania, J., 41
Schafft, K., 8, 11, 23, 51, 65, 87, 93
Schmuck, P., 95
Schmuck, R., 95
School Administrators Association of New York, 64
school choice, 66
Schools Under Registration Review (SURR), 66, 67, 68
Schulte, A., 6
Scott, J., 8, 116
Scribner, C. F., 96
SEED grant program, 81
Seelig, J. L., 5, 7, 78
Self, T., 86
self-studies, 6
Shaw, N., 86
Sherman, J., 5, 23, 48, 51, 77, 80, 87, 90, 95
Sipple, J. W., 11, 65, 80, 93, 95
Slentz, Ken, 64
Smarsh, S., 23
Smith, Alfred, 60
Smith, P. J., 109
social media, 48, 49

Spaulding, Francis, 61, 108
Special Education Quality Assurance (SEQA), 29
Spitzer, Elliot, 63, 76
Stachowski, William, 79
standardized testing as an indicator, 22
Stanley, L., 83
State University of New York (SUNY) system, 41, 65, 106
St. Bonaventure, 106
Steele, J., 19
Stein, A., 112
students, teachers' impacts on, 7, 83
subaltern research, 8–9
Suozzi, Thomas, 63
Suozzi Commission, 76
superintendents: district, 30; recruitment and turnover as indicators, 24–25; salary discussions in the Herkimer County case study, 43–44; sharing of, 72; and teacher retention, 81; use of comparisons, 31
Sutherland, D. H., 107

Tangorra, C., 8, 19
Teacher Improvement Fund grants, 68
teachers: impacts on rural students, 7; recruitment and turnover as indicators, 23–24; retention of, 78–79, 80–81; salary discussions in the Herkimer County case study, 44; and student perceptions of school value, 83; in suburban school districts, 24, 80; use of comparisons, 31–32; viewed as low-level service workers, 44–45
Tech Valley High School program (P-TECH), 72
Theobald, P., 6, 23, 46, 65, 93, 96
thick descriptions, 7

Thier, M., 3, 5, 10, 118
Thomas, A. R., 1, 5, 65, 80, 93, 105, 107, 108, 112, 116
Tibout theory, 77
Tieken, M. C., 8, 65, 93, 95, 97
Timberline School District case study, 99–101
Tinkham, J., 89, 90
Trujillo, K., 36
Trump, Donald, 1, 10
trust, lack of, 43, 45–46, 48, 54, 101–2
Turner, F. J., 81
Twain, Mark, 106
Tyack, D. B., 62

urbanormativity, 1, 59, 90–91, 107–8, 116
urban school policy, 66–69

Vance, J. D., 107

Walker-Gibbs, B., 6, 89
Warren, M., 43
Weis, Lois, 45, 93
West, M., 86–87
Westfield Academy and Central School District. *See* Brocton-Westfield case study
wicked problem concept, 89–90, 117
Wildavsky, A., 40
Willis, P., 83
Winner Commission, 79, 80
Wood, K., 96
Working Class Without Work (Weis), 45
Wuthnow, R., 2, 108

Yinger, J., 20, 40
Yun, J. T., 67

Zuckerman, S. J., 65, 90

About the Author

Dr. **Casey Thomas Jakubowski** (PhD, Education Policy and Leadership, SUNY Albany) holds a certificate in mentoring teachers (University at Buffalo), a Masters of Arts, History (Binghamton) and is a proud graduate of SUNY Fredonia (BA, Social Studies Education). Currently teaching the University of Maryland Eastern Shore doctorate in education program, his research focuses on rural education and rural history, sociology, citizenship, and civics education.

The author of three other books (*Thinking About Teaching*, *A Cog in the Machine*, and *HEARTS*) and coauthor of *Crush It from the Start: 50 Tips for New Teachers*, all focused on the education recruitment, retention, and practice, with a rural focus. Casey's academic work has appeared in international, national, regional, and state-level journals and at conferences. Dr. Jakubowski is the founder of CTJ Solutions, LLC and a co-principal at Alpine Peak Consulting.